HIS DOUGH, HER COOKIE

HIS DOUGH, HER COOKIE

THE BLACK WOMAN'S GUIDE TO LOVE AND MARRIAGE IN THE AGE OF INDEPENDENCE

TORRI STUCKEY

COVER THREE PUBLISHING
UNITED STATES

His Dough, *Her* Cookie

Published by Cover Three Publishing
P.O. Box 947, Oak Forest, IL 60452-0947

Copyright © 2017 by Torri Stuckey

ISBN: 9780692729458

Printed in the United States of America
2017—First Edition

Edited by Carol Taylor
Cover photo by Corey Hanks
Cover design by Denise Billups
Interior design by Matt Duckett
Indexed by Laura Shelley

*To my wife, Leanne,
and children Zoe, Caleb and Tori*

CONTENTS

Make every effort to change things you do not like. If you cannot make a change, change the way you have been thinking.
You might find a new solution.

—Maya Angelou

INTRODUCTION

Not Yo' Mama's Relationship Book

I promised myself that I would never write a book about relationships. There are more than enough home-wrecking handbooks in the marketplace—to the point of saturation. Walk into any bookstore and look around you. Most walls are trimmed with relationship advice rather than wainscoting.

Obviously, not all relationship books are "home-wrecking." However, they all have the potential to be. They all make a similar detrimental suggestion…conformity. Many encourage you—directly or indirectly—to alter your relationship structure, and make your relationship fit a mold. Once the relationship contours to that mold, it indicates the relationship is "healthy."

In reality, relationships are as unique as the people in them. The more unique they are, the harder it is for them to conform to a conventional relationship model. But a unique relationship by no means signifies an ill-fated one; simply an unorthodox one.

Relationship books are dangerous because people don't dictate relationships, patterns do—be they positive or negative. These patterns help shape the relationship's dynamics. These dynamics are exclusive to that specific relationship; because patterns change from relationship to relationship. Not only do patterns change, but people change from one relationship to the next. This further un-

3

derscores the peril of one-size-fits-all relationship advice.

If one partner in the relationship tries to implement a new or different pattern, it changes the dynamic of the relationship and often creates conflict. For example, in a relationship where the woman wears the pants, but after much ridicule from his friends the man tries to exercise some authority and seize control, right or wrong, this attempted coup will create conflict and cause problems.

Conflict, at its extreme, can destroy a relationship. Couples in relationships that have withstood the test of time—understand this phenomenon and so have been able to weather the storm. Both, the man and woman use the conflict as a way to strengthen their bond rather than tear it apart.

This helps explain why a marriage between two young God-fearing Christians can end in divorce in less than three years, meanwhile the union between two life-long swingers can go on for thirty years and counting... The key to longevity is establishing common beliefs and determining what works best for your particular relationship. I acknowledge that sometimes you're too close to the relationship to look at it objectively. Outside advice can be helpful and provide much needed fresh perspective. Just remember, no matter how close they are to you, people outside of your relationship will never understand all its nuances.

Sometimes, outside advice is like getting a second opinion from a doctor without giving him your complete medical information. He'll diagnose you based on historical trends rather than your specific medical history. This is a surefire way to be misdiagnosed. By the same token, outside advice via books or family and friends is a surefire way to create a cancer within your relationship, especially if you're seeking advice before you're even certain of your own desires and goals for the relationship.

What is the goal of a relationship? Ultimately, I believe we're all looking for two key components: happiness and longevity. Longevity is simply finding a way to keep both people inside the love boat and rowing in the same direction. That doesn't mean either of you pretends problems don't exist. It means you both constructively work through them. Avoiding conflict by sweeping issues under the rug might increase longevity; however, it's likely that one, or both of you will be unhappy. At some point this unhappiness will manifest itself in some form of destructive behavior; such as abuse, an affair, alcoholism, apathy or even alienation.

Happiness looks different for everyone. It's complex and ever-changing, depending on internal and external influences. What brings you happiness in the early stages of a relationship may drastically change as the relationship matures. This emphasizes the importance of growing together with your partner. In the absence of growing together you grow apart. You wake up one day feeling like the walls of the relationship are closing in on you. Many people say they've "fallen out of love." It's more likely that the relationship is no longer on one accord.

What separates *HDHC* from traditional relationship books? It comes from a place of and for Black love. As a Black community activist, my motive is simple. I desire prosperity for Black people— both socially and financially. I view Black women as the gatekeepers and lynchpins of the Black community, and the success of that community hinges on Black women rediscovering their intrinsic value in the community and restoring the balance of power.

HDHC takes a broad look at Black relationships (or lack thereof), focusing specifically on the role Black women play as the catalyst in rebuilding the Black community. It is as much an observation as it is an analysis.

For example, later in the book I will decree that if you are a Black woman who cares about the strength of the Black community, the greatest deed you can do for it is to marry a Black man. I offer this advice despite population data that suggests you will be significantly reducing your chances for love because my advice is not specific to individuals; it's community-focused. When broadening the scope statistics support my assertion, whether it's Black household wealth, Black men's career success, or Black population growth.

I classify this book as a Black empowerment manifesto disguised as relationship advice. My desire to meddle in Black women's dating lives only extends to the degree in which it impacts the Black community. I have a deep affinity for urban Black America. Empowering and uplifting it has become a lifelong focus. I hold tightly to the belief that one day all Black communities in this nation will have the economic prowess to sustain themselves.

Eagerly desiring financial freedom for the Black community has been frustrating, painful and vexing. Few economic indicators suggest we are heading in the right direction. In fact, some suggest we are losing ground. The wealth gap between Black and White households has drastically increased over the past decade.

There are a myriad of issues permeating the Black community. Among them, drugs, gangs, violence, illiteracy, and disenfranchisement, are retarding its growth and perpetuating the cycle of poverty from generation to generation. However, I view none more pervasive or paramount than fatherless homes.

According to statistics, 72 percent of Black babies are born to unmarried mothers. An overwhelming figure, clearly indicating we've reached epidemic proportions. Yet on the surface, it appears the Black community has accepted this flagrant indiscretion. Inexcusably, the unwed birth percentage has almost tripled in the Black community since the 1960s. How did we arrive at a point in Black society where we've identified fatherless homes as a debilitating problem, but the community has grown too jaded to care?

My strong conviction is that Black women as a whole have relinquished their power and rightful place in Black society through the birth of the Independent Black Woman, a financially stable woman who provides for herself and is proud of her ability to stand alone, and subsequent death of the institution of marriage—creating a new social (dis)order. As a result, Black women find themselves at the precipice of a self-fulfilling prophecy, while the Black community deteriorates due to this social dysfunction.

With increasingly more Black women declaring their independence and one in three Black men expected to go to prison, if the problem is not addressed, there soon may be no remnant or semblance of a Black community left to salvage.

My theory may seem counterintuitive. Without question many Black women will feel as if I'm preaching to the choir, "Black women are already clocking overtime on their jobs," they will say. I agree. Still they shoulder equal culpability.

The plight of Black men has been well documented in other books, articles and the like. Periodically relationship books venture to turn the microscope onto Black women to be scrutinized under magnification. Yet none have analyzed the role Black women

7

have played in the demise of the Black family and subsequently the Black community.

My sincere hope is to ignite a national dialogue on the fundamental roles of Black women within the Black family and community. I pray this book helps my Black sistahs set aside preconceived thoughts about marriage and challenge them to develop their own. I hope it inspires them to take a deeper look at the critical part they play in turning the tide and setting the course for Black America.

By no means am I attempting to alienate Black men—or castrate them for that matter. The success of the Black community is binary. Black men are equally important. However, they are not equally as present, which has created generations of children who don't know their father. No matter the plausible reasons why, it's hard to be a change agent if you are absent. Considering the current climate, deliberate steps must be taken by Black women to preserve the future of the Black community and Black race. *His Dough, Her Cookie* seeks to highlight and outline some of these steps.

THE PROBLEM

"HOUSTON—One recent day at Dr. Natalie Carroll's OB-GYN practice, located inside a low-income apartment complex tucked between a gas station and a freeway, 12 pregnant Black women come for consultations. Some bring their children or their mothers. Only one brings a husband."—*Jesse Washington, The Associated Press*

Are 42 Percent of Black Women Unwed?

Are Black women disproportionately single? Depending on whom you ask you'll receive varying opinions in stark contradistinction. This inquiry started with a study conducted in 2009 by two researchers at Yale University. Based on their research, the study concluded that 42 percent of Black women eighteen years and older have never been married—double the percentage of White women who've yet to marry.

Since the Yale publication, Black scholars and activists alike have made it their chief focus to ambush this study. Several counter studies, articles and reports have been published. All attempting to find inaccuracies to discredit the original study.

Some of these scholars maintain that the numbers have been manipulated by the media and other opportunistic factions to further exacerbate a negative image of Black America for the sole purpose of exploitation. They argue, if one simply changes the starting age in the analysis from eighteen and older to thirty-five and older, the percent of Black women who have never been married drops to 25 percent.

My question is "Why thirty-five years of age?" It appears to be as arbitrary as eighteen. There are sixteen other starting points between eighteen and thirty-five that could've been used. Were they deceptively excluded because they too paint a negative picture? Re-gardless, even if thirty-five is used as the starting point, the percent of unwed Black women drops to 25 percent; however, that number is still double the percentage of White women using the same start-ing point.

Other Black scholars regard these statistics as an anti-Black ploy. They point out that women, regardless of race, are marrying at a lesser rate; yet turn a blind eye to the fact that lack of marriage within the Black community is responsible for the increasing eco-nomic and social inequality, reflected by the wealth gap continuing to widen between Black and White families. They reduce the num-bers to nothing more than a scare tactic used by the media to cre-ate panic and mass hysteria within the Black community—keeping Black men and women at variance. The rest of us live in the real world.

We've witnessed, firsthand, the adversarial relationship between Black men and women that predates any panic induced by this study. Regardless, acknowledging that White people are marrying at a lesser rate when the conversation is specifically discussing the fate of marriage in the Black community is parallel to someone insisting that "All Lives Matter" in response to "Black Lives Matter."

You would be hard pressed to find a greater critic of the media than me. I take advantage of every opportunity to point out their flaws. I concede there is clearly a bias in the way news is report-ed in mainstream media, which often portrays Black America in a disparaging way. However, I disagree with that designation for this state of affairs.

When there are diverging opinions and inconclusive evidence to support an argument, I set aside all the analytics and move from

12

a quantitative measurement to a more qualitative one. I rely on a basic human sense to guide me to a belief. I'm referring to none other than the age-old smell test. It may seem archaic and unsophisticated, but it is simple and effective. If it doesn't pass the smell test, I don't believe it. If it smells like bull$**t, it likely is.

Asking a man who was raised by a single mother, whose mother was raised by a single mother, whose entire circle of childhood friends came from single-mother homes and whose current male mentoring group consists of young men being raised by single mothers, to believe the media is somehow cooking the data to push an agenda and there is no real cause for concern is not only futile, but also foolish.

Beyond the 42 percent is the more significant, less debated statistic mentioned earlier, noting that 72 percent of Black babies are born to unmarried mothers (in comparison to 24 percent of White babies). Without question this number includes some children whose parents chose not to marry, but nonetheless live together under one roof and are products of a healthy and stable family structure. Still the majority of children in these circumstances are living in households without a father—an estimated 67 percent. This is the root of most problems in Black America. Financial disadvantages notwithstanding, the social and emotional ills are immeasurable: depression, substance abuse, premature sexuality, teen pregnancy, anti-social behavior, crime and juvenile delinquency. Statistics indicate accelerated levels of all areas in fatherless homes relative to two-parent homes. The Black community cannot heal and rid itself of ills until we heal the Black family.

The first step in recovery is admitting there is a problem. To borrow a line from a popular nineties rap song "Ain't No Future In

Yo Frontin'." Those Black male scholars who sing Black women's praises are said to truly love and respect them. However, if one is incapable of thinking critically about Black women's issues, both internal and external, if one is completely unwilling to acknowledge the ugly, then turn it upside down and examine its underbelly and suggest ways Black women can be better, that's not love. It's pacification.

I have a deep affinity for Black women, so much that I've never dated outside of my race. It's not a prejudice. It's a preference. I prefer everything about a Black woman more than any other race: her style, her grace, her strength, her beauty, her intelligence, her depth, her curves and sex appeal. This is why I married one. But when you truly love someone, you're honest with them even when it hurts. I don't hate Black women; I love them enough to tell the truth.

As a Black community, in general, we have to own up to our faults. Let's stop sweeping our dirt under the rug and rejecting statistics that don't fit the narrative we prefer to tell. Some Black scholars are fighting to preserve the façade of a healthy relationship between Black men and women, while the Black community is hemorrhaging from the lack thereof.

My last book *Impoverished State of Mind* created a similar response from some in the Black scholar community. Suggesting that beyond physical poverty, there is an issue with the mindset of many Black people living in poverty that prevents them from rising above it, meant I had crossed over to the other side. I now had a conservative right-wing view of poverty that suggests it is merely a state of mind—that Black people just need to take ownership of their lives and stop playing the role of victim. This couldn't be further from the truth. I went out of my way to point out the outside forces working against the Black community to hinder growth. However, I didn't stop there as many Black scholars do; I introduced the idea that there are internal focuses that are also hindering growth. The two are not mutually exclusive. I used data to connect the dots.

Accepting a statistic doesn't mean you live your life according to it. However, it's helpful to understand the odds you are up against. Understanding them can help you better circumvent the murky waters or navigate through the tough terrain, as you grind to prosperity individually and we work toward success collectively.

Where Did It Go Wrong?

Theories behind the devaluing of marriage within the Black community are vast: birth of the Independent Black Woman, the hip-hop era effect, and skyrocketing divorce rates, for instance. Some scholars link the onset to as far back as slavery, when marriage was prohibited, fathers were often sold off, and mother and child separated—all never to be reunited. Proponents of this theory argue that what Blacks are experiencing today is a complex residual effect caused by the deconstruction of family during the slave era.

An expressive firsthand description of the effects of slavery on families can be felt in the hopeless words of Hannah Valentine—slave, wife and mother of seven. In a letter written to her husband Michael, Hannah expresses her despair over the breaking up of their family.

Both Hannah and Michael were owned by the Campbell fam-

15

ily—David and Mary. Hannah was sold to the Campbell family in 1811 when she was only seventeen years old. Hannah was made a servant. She and other servants lived in the basement of the main house. A lifelong house Negro, Hannah eventually became manager of the house servants.

Michael was purchased fifteen years later and became David Campbell's trusted carriage driver. Though ten years her junior, Michael and Hannah would marry shortly after his arrival.

David Campbell served as governor of Virginia during the period of this letter (1837-1840). Once elected, he and his family moved into the governor's mansion in the state capital (Richmond). Michael and several of his and Hannah's children were among the servants brought to the mansion. Hannah was left behind in Abingdon to tend to the Campbell estate, as well as her grandchildren— Eliza's brood.

Though she would learn to read and write in her lifetime, Historians believe this letter was written for Hannah by young men prior to her literacy. Even if the letter was produced through a surrogate, the raw emotions are authentic.

Abingdon, VA January 30, 1838

My dear husband

I begin to feel so anxious to hear from you and my children, and indeed from all the family that I have concluded to write to you altho you have treated me badly in not answering my last letter. I heard through Mr Gibson last week that you were all well, but hearing from you in that way does not satisfy me. I want a letter to tell me what you are doing and all about yourself and Eliza & David. Mr Nat Barker sent to let me know that he would set off to Richmond in the stage to day, but I could not get my letter ready in time for home this morning, but if he has put it off until the next stage, as I think he probably has I can still send it by him, or if he is gone, by mail. ... Tell Eliza her children grow very fast. They do not talk much about her now, but seem to be very well satisfied without her. I begin to feel anxious to see you all. I am afraid my patience will be quite worn out if you do not come back soon. You must write and tell me when Master talks of returning, and when you write tell me particularly about Master & Mistress how they look and if Mistress is as much pleased with Richmond as at first. ... Tell David I am much pleased to hear that he has been a good boy. he must continue to be so, and tell him he must send me a message in you next letter. Give my love to Eliza and tell her she must write to me. I want o hear hoe she gets along without her Mammy to help her. Give my best love to Master & Mistress and to Miss Virginia, Give my love to Richard & David, and believe me always you affectionate wife.

Hannah Valentine

How beautifully tragic are her words? How perfectly apropos her surname? A symphony of emotions resonating through every word, confessing her love while expressing her anguish. Perhaps the most heart-wrenching yet hope-inspiring dagger delivered was when she informed her daughter, Eliza, that Eliza's children no longer mentioned their mother. They've grown to find fulfillment despite her absence—a bittersweet reality for many Black slaves.

Though marriage was unlawful, at the master's discretion, slaves could be joined in union. Since both Michael and Hannah were owned by the Campbell family, they were permitted to marry

17

in the eyes of God. Considered a civil right, marriage was only available to free people. For Black slaves, marriage was a symbolic gesture of their commitment, and included such acts as jumping the broom—a common ritual used to consecrate slave marriages.

> After while I was taken a notion to marry, and Massa and Missy marries us same as all the niggers. They stands inside the house with a broom held crosswise of the door, and we stands outside. Missy puts a li'l wreath on my head they kept there, and we steps over the broom into the the house. Now, that's all they was to the marryin'. After freedom I gits married and has it put in the book by a preacher.
>
> Ex-slave Mary Reynolds

Contrary to popular belief, many slaves married—by their master or with their master's consent. It's been substantiated by many firsthand accounts. Not to be misconstrued was masters' motive for allowing marriage. This was far from an altruistic gesture. It was a business decision. Marriage provided security for slave owners. It served as asset protection and loss prevention.

Whip a slave until submission, then continue to whip him to set an example for all others. Make a slave's life intolerable yet comfortable enough that he finds refuge in the plush white cotton fields of the plantation. Allow him to experience love and relative happiness. Let his unending hope be a semblance of life as a freeman, that way he'll remain in place—never trying to escape.

If you place a frog in a pot of boiling water, it will leap out immediately. However, if you place the frog in lukewarm water and gradually increase the temperature, it won't try to flee. By the time the frog realizes what is happening, it's already frog soup.

There are reports of some slaves being forcefully married or at least required to mate. Slaves were property. This act falls under the same practice as forced breeding of cattle, horses and other farm animals. Its only purpose was to create more livestock.

There was a preponderance of voluntary slave marriages. Slave families understood the importance of relationships beyond monetary dimensions. It was deeply rooted in their West African heritage. They recognized the vital role of family to their own survival. Family, faith and freedom are the overarching themes in letters and songs from the slave era, but the greatest of these was family. Their love of family was deep and abiding, causing many to put themselves at grave risk in order to preserve its integrity, and sometimes be put to death as punishment for trying.

Post-Civil War, once Blacks could legally marry, many took advantage of this civil liberty. They exercised this right with great eagerness. According to African American historian Tera Hunter, it was "to the point of overwhelming the Union Army, making it very difficult for them to handle the numbers of people trying to get married." This imagery of former slaves rushing to the altar is why numerous Black scholars believe the rumors of slavery's impact have been grossly exaggerated—sneering at the notion that the antebellum holds the answers to the degradation of Black love.

One would be hard pressed to deny slavery complicated marriage and Black family dynamics in ways that shook it to its core. Fathers had no paternal rights. Mother's rights were extended modestly so long as they didn't jeopardize the business of the south or infringe on White supremacy.

Despite the deconstruction of marriage during slavery, marriage was all but ubiquitous among Blacks by the 1900s. Family relationships notably improved, but they were never fully restored. Beyond the measurable number of marriages lay deeper structural damage that would resurface half a century later. The Black community was no longer operating under a patriarchal landscape. As a result of Black males being sold off or slaughtered, Black women took the helm as the leader of the family as well as the community, shifting the paradigm and creating a matriarchal system.

The Great Debacle

Today, many Blacks look to the Civil Rights Era as our glory days, yearning to have been a part of it. However, it was in its midst that Black families started falling apart again. The "Redestruction Era" of Black families began in 1963 with the presidency of Lyndon B. Johnson (LBJ). Former Vice President, Johnson was sworn in as the 36th U.S. president after the assassination of John F. Kennedy. Johnson would later outright win the presidency in 1964 with 61 percent of the vote. As a former senator, Johnson was considered to have conservative views (i.e., voting record); however, he seemingly detached from them and affixed to his liberal roots during his presidency.

Johnson's campaign ran on a platform declaring a "war on poverty." He promised to take action against the social albatrosses perpetuating the cycle of poverty in our nation to create a better America. LBJ quickly delivered on his promises. Shortly after being sworn in, he successfully negotiated one of the most expansive domestic programs in U.S. history. His legislative agenda became widely known as the "Great Society." Johnson's vision of the Great Society can best be described through his own words. In a 1964 speech addressing the University of Michigan, Johnson proclaimed:

> The Great Society rests on abundance and liberty for all. It demands an end to poverty and racial injustice, to which we are totally committed in our time. But that is just the beginning.
>
> The Great Society is a place where every child can find knowledge to enrich his mind and to enlarge his talents. It is a place where leisure is a welcome chance to build and reflect, not a feared cause of boredom and restlessness. It is a place where the city of man serves not only the needs of the body and the demands of commerce but the desire for beauty and hunger for community.
>
> It is a place where man can renew contact with nature. It is a place which honors creation for its own sake and for what it adds to the understanding of the race. It is a place where men are more concerned with the quality of their goals than the quantity of their goods.
>
> But most of all, the Great Society is not a safe harbor, a resting place, a final objective, a finished work. It is a challenge constantly renewed, beckoning us toward a destiny where the meaning of our lives matches the marvelous products of our labor.

Johnson portrayed the Great Society as a magical place. Ultimately, it would prove to be a mythical one, a mere ideal that was left unattended, and that which caused decades of injury to Black families.

The Great Society focused primarily on poverty, which by virtue equated Black people, since Blacks were dis-proportionately poor. In May of 1965, Johnson launched Project Head Start through the Office of Economic Opportunity—which he established to oversee his agenda. Head Start began as an eight-week summer program for preschool children from low-income communities. It was designed to address the achievement gap, providing an underserved population of children with a broad program to meet their academic, health, nutritional and psychological needs. The program provided preschool classes, medical care, dental care, and mental health services.

Job Corps, a residential training and employment program designed to address the myriad of obstacles to employment faced by disadvantaged youth, came into existence as a result of LBJ's Great Society. Johnson signed into law the Voting Rights Act of 1965 which prohibited racial discrimination in voting. The Social Security Amendments of 1965 which created Medicaid, a program providing healthcare to low-income families and individuals, and Medicare which provided health insurance for the elderly and poor families. The Elementary and Secondary Education Act of 1965 (better known as Title 1), affording federal funds to be provided to public schools in an effort to ensure all children have an equal opportunity to obtain a quality education.

In my estimation, LBJ's Great Society made vast improvements, which helped catapult the nation into a new era of liberalism in America that was both notable and applause worthy. Where his agenda fell short or crossed the line, depending on how you look at it, was in the expanded resources for welfare: food stamps, public housing, child care assistance and cash aid. This had a catastrophically adverse effect.

An attempt was made by Daniel Patrick Moynihan to warn Johnson of the potential ramifications of knee-jerk legislation prior to enactment; however, those warnings fell on deaf ears. On his own accord, Moynihan, the Assistant Secretary of Labor, soliciting help from his staff created a report on the Black family titled *The Negro Family: The Case for National Action*. It would later be infamously branded the "Moynihan Report" and be etched in history as one of the most provocative writings of its era.

Moynihan, a Navy veteran, set sail on a mission to prove to the Johnson administration that racial equality could not be achieved via civil rights legislation alone. He insisted that more "affirmative" action was necessary along with some sort of social correctness that addresses the mind state of the Negro people who over three centuries have been conditioned to be subordinate. Freedom without opportunity would leave Negroes in a position of dependency. Opportunity without reconditioning would leave Negroes preferring dependency. This is how an initiative like the Great Society that so clearly focused on the progressing of the Black community ultimately resulted in its decimation.

First, the execution and deployment of the funds were subpar; in typical government fashion legislators threw millions of dollars at the problem without clear oversight. People figured out how to "work the system." Program recipients became abusive, taking resources that were strictly supplemental and turning them into primary sources of income. Poor Blacks became caught in the snares of welfare. Places like public housing projects, designed as a temporary dwelling to subsidize living expenses giving the lower class an opportunity to better save for a permanent home, became their final resting place.

As a product of public housing, I know the storyline all too well. Over time, single mothers become married to welfare, for better or worse, until death. It is an arranged marriage organized by the U.S. government that some feel is a conspiracy to keep Blacks as second-class citizens. At the least, the government is guilty of negligence in the appropriation and oversight of funds.

Every decision has unintended consequences. The government's myopic lens left them defenseless against the adverse social issues in Black families that arose from the new robust welfare programs. The expansion of welfare through the Food Stamp Act of 1964 and Housing and Urban Development Act of 1965 disrupted God's natural family order, emasculating Black fathers and placing supreme power in the hands of Black mothers through fiscal fortification. Mothers could now stand alone. And alone they stood— independent and proud. Family needs not covered by their hourly wages were supplemented by government assistance. Black fathers became irrelevant—a nuisance even.

Welfare benefits discouraged low-income Black couples from marrying. It created a quandary for Black women, an ultimatum that essentially encouraged them to "choose government over husband." Marriage carried severe financial ramifications. It would mean relinquishing some if not all government assistance and potentially producing a net loss, as benefits varied based on total household income. Exchanging a virtually fixed income at the risk of Black fathers' employment security was hardly a prudent trade-off. For Black mothers, marriage meant conceding both money *and* power.

Another unforeseen issue caused by welfare policies and procedures is the criminalization of Black fathers. In order to receive welfare assistance mothers are required to report the identity of the child's father, instituting child support responsibilities against the father and giving the government legal rights to recoup funds provided to mothers through welfare benefits. Desperate to escape child support payments, lots of fathers work less profitable pay-under-the-table jobs. As they fall delinquent on child support, many find themselves in legal troubles punishable by prison, further fueling an adversarial relationship between Black mothers and fathers.

When you reward a certain behavior, you only get more of it. In the ten years following the launch of the Great Society the percentage of single Black mothers doubled. By 1994 that number had tripled, ballooning from 24 percent in 1964 to 70 percent in 1994. Not to mention the domino effect it caused producing a generation of Black girls raised in single-mother homes, turned Black women who suffer from symptoms of fatherlessness and have no appreciation for fatherhood. They too dismiss the value of needing the father in the home. They judge the value of a partner in terms of financial contribution to the household. With lucrative careers or public welfare affording the ability to provide for their family, a father's presence becomes a luxury not a necessity.

Today, you have a single-mother dichotomy that has formed between the educated professional Black mom, who is thriving in Corporate America, and the undereducated, working class Black mom, surviving off waitress tips and welfare—with the latter giving birth at a much higher rate. To speak about Black women as a whole appears as though I'm conflating the issues, with the two in stark contrast to each other. One producing significantly less burden from a government and taxpayer standpoint; however, from an independent woman or fatherless home perspective, they are creating like consequences for their offspring. Every child's suffering looks different, but they are suffering all the same.

The debate surrounding the epicenter of the Black families' destruction is left to interpretation. Some Black intellectuals believe the effects of slavery have been exaggerated. Others stand firm in their conviction that the Great Society is ground zero. I don't view the issue as an either-or situation. Collectively, both negatively impacted the Black family. The aftershocks are still being felt.

Today, few Blacks can identify with slavery, but many can identify with being poor—a byproduct of slavery. The disproportionate need for welfare and government assistance to Blacks is in part a result of slavery, causing LBJ to declare a war on poverty. Therefore, the two are not juxtaposed; they are forever connected.

THE ARGUMENT

What Came First the Dough or the Cookie?

Sadly, many intimate relationships have been reduced to transactions—women desiring his dough and men lusting after her cookie—without either having a true understanding of the relationship between dough and cookie.

Dough is to cookie what man is to woman. How so? A cookie could not exist if not for the dough and dough is not complete in its raw form. Woman would not exist if not for man and man is not complete without woman. The unified relationship between the two is explained in the first book of the Bible.

> The Lord God said, "It is not good for the man to be alone. I will make a helper suitable for him." ... So the Lord God caused the man [Adam] to fall into a deep sleep; and while he was sleeping, he took one of the man's ribs and then closed up the place with flesh. Then the Lord God made a woman from the rib he had taken out of the man, and he brought her to the man. The man said, "This is now bone of my bones and flesh of my flesh; she shall be called 'woman,' for she was taken out of man." This is why a man leaves his father and mother and is united to his wife, and they become one flesh.
>
> Genesis 2:18-23

29

Often misinterpreted, being "one flesh" consists of more than the physical act of sex. It's sharing life beyond the superficial physical and material aspects: smiles and cries, feats and failures, dreams and fears, joys and pains, comforts and sufferings. Ultimately, man and woman are designed to come together in marriage to form a sacred oneness—becoming one soul as well as one body.

Marriage, as God ordained it, between one man and one woman is designed for man to be the head of the household. This is not a social norm. It represents man and woman's natural equilibrium. This organic relationship has been misaligned through the growth of the Independent Black Woman. Black women went from being the backbone of the family and community, placing value on taking care of home and building community, to pinning their ears back and chasing money like men. They've been very successful in doing so. However, the ramifications of their actions have been costly consequences for which, not even a six-figure salary can compensate.

One could even make the argument that Black mothers have essentially become absent in the home, as well as the community, and society would be none the wiser. Ultimately, the absence of Black fathers largely overshadows the deficiencies of Black mothers, giving the impression of a satisfactory grade—when measured against the "dad curve." But Black women, to a certain degree, have abandoned the idea of family and community in exchange for individual money and power.

I want to be careful not to confuse the desire of Black women to be successful career women with the desire to be independent. Contrary to the popular belief, the two are not synonymous. Having a career can provide financial independence, but it in and of itself does not make someone an independent woman. Even being forced into prolonged singledom or single motherhood doesn't make you an independent woman. Being an independent woman is a mindset wherein you prefer or choose to be sovereign and stand alone. It's a state of mind rooted in fear and produced by pain and disappointment from past experiences.

The issue is not Black women having a career. I'm not clamoring for us to step back into the '50s and have Black women walk around the kitchen barefoot and pregnant. I'm suggesting that the end goal should be marriage (i.e., togetherness) not independence. White women have had tremendous success in the corporate world. I've yet to hear any refer to themselves as an "Independent White Woman." Despite their success most still value marriage.

Now that Black women have their own money, the playing field has been leveled from a financial perspective, giving them the ability to say to Black men "I don't need you!" Prosperity has given Black women a false sense of power and a cocky "never put a man before my money" attitude. The caricature of the strong Independent Black Woman has saturated mass media, from advertisements to television shows to song lyrics.

Black women have created several self-empowering terms of endearment: power woman, girl boss, boss babe, lady boss among others, to declare their female prowess. Books such as Amber Rose's *How to Be a Bad Bitch* further exacerbates the issue. This is even more aggravating since Rose doesn't identify as being Black but has been adopted by Black America because of her hip-hop ties. Last but not least, we have Beyoncé and her fanatical Beyhive following running around fist pumping and shouting "Who run the world? Girls!" While this pseudo feminist/quasi-chauvinist rhetoric might serve as much needed motivation for young independent Black women, carrying this self-sufficient, egotistical attitude into a relationship is disastrous.

The term "power couple" has been coined to denote a couple where the woman is earning a lucrative salary alongside her man. However, this "power" for women is finite. In a marriage, woman cannot assume an authority that has been bestowed upon man by our creator. Some view these thoughts as sexist and patriarchal, aimed to keep women living as second-class citizens. As a citizen of the kingdom, I view it as God's holy ordinance. However, these laws are not limited to Christians alone. Man's inherent characteristics, combined with defined social norms, place all relationships operating outside of this decree in harm's way.

Several years ago I was having a conversation and informal counseling session with a friend who was having serious relationship problems with his girlfriend of seven years. They'd been living together the entire time, for all intents and purposes operating under common-law marriage.

"What's been the common theme of your arguments?" I asked.

"Finances," he answered without hesitation.

"Do you guys have a joint checking account to pay your bills?"

"Nope."

"Why not?" I asked. "It's a great way to keep track of your spending and budget accordingly. One of the first things we did when we got married was open a joint checking account. We pay all our bills online through it. Then, we take a monthly allowance from it for our personal checking. It's been smooth."

"I know. But Leslie ain't goin' for that."

"So how do y'all handle bills?"

"She takes care of the bills she's responsible for and I take care of the ones I'm responsible for."

"But y'all live together and share a child. You're both equally responsible for all the bills. It sounds like you're both hanging on to a single person's mentality when you're now a team. It's not her money or your money anymore. It's the family's money."

"I don't have a problem with a joint account. But Leslie will."

"Well, as the man of the house, make the executive decision for the family and schedule an appointment at the bank."

"It's easy for you to say. You're the sole breadwinner of the house. You know Leslie. She ain't no pushover. Bottom line, she makes more money than me. Significantly more! So how can I make her?"

His words stunned me like a Taser. I sat in shock for five minutes, blown away by how vulnerable he was in that moment. Even more amazing was the fact that he seemed fully invested in his beliefs, browbeaten by this emasculating ideology that her higher salary somehow entitled her to supreme authority.

Realizing where he was mentally, I backed off and didn't press the issue. My goal was to help reduce conflict not create more. If he could accept his role, no matter how reluctantly, who was I to disrupt their dynamic? I watched as they struggled through the relationship, until he decided to end it eleven months later.

His Dough v. *Her* Cookie

Despite their growing independence, two aspects of life a Black woman cannot provide for herself are companionship and intimacy. So begins the game of his dough v. her cookie. Because no matter how much money a woman amasses, she will always prefer her man has at least as much, if not more, in the bank. Women like for men to provide. Real men like to be providers. It gives us a sense of pride. These innate characteristics are the reasons a wealthy man will date a broke woman, but a rich woman will virtually never date a poor man. This is also why a woman is willing to date men ten years her senior if he is "more established," which is a euphemism for "financially stable" and why these older men will oblige.

These patterns further illustrate that the natural order of men and women has been disrupted in the Black community. God never intended for relationships to be complicated. He provided an order—man as the head and woman as the helper. Despite how much society tries to deviate from this foundation, there will always be signs we are operating outside of our natural origin. The alarming statistic that 42 percent of Black women are unwed and 72 percent of Black children are being born out of wedlock, is more than a sign. It's a billboard!

Shortly after the 2009 Yale study that suggested 42 percent of Black women over eighteen were unwed was released, speculation started as to why there was such a high percentage of unmarried Black women. Why a percentage that is *double* the figure of their White counterparts? The theories have been endless, ranging from intuitive to ridiculous. However, a general consensus by most ex-

34

perts is that the problem can be segmented into six categories: population disparities, incarceration rates, interracial dating, education gap, joblessness and homosexuality.

The population argument simply states that from a childbirth perspective, there is a 3:1 ratio of girls to boys born in America, creating a natural deficit. At present, there are roughly 1.9 million more Black women than Black men. Per these gender statistics, if every Black bachelor wedded a Black bride, one in twelve Black women would still be hard pressed to find a husband.

This statistic is further exacerbated by Black women's greater unwillingness to date or marry outside of their race than Black men. Interracial dating between Blacks and Whites has increased in general with Black men and White women being the most common pair. This dynamic further cultivates an environment that produces scarcity among available Black men, leaving Black women to sift through a dwindling dating pool in search of love.

The new millennium brought about new press on an age-old issue of Black male incarceration and the racial disparities in the American criminal justice system. Not to be overshadowed is how mass incarceration affects the availability of the Black male. The New Jim Crow theory, made popular by author Michelle Alexander, basically argues there are more Black males under criminal justice control (incarcerated, parole or probation) today than were enslaved in 1860. Beyond the barbed wire and brick walls of lockdown, Black men find themselves locked out of job opportunities on the outside as a result of felony records—making more Black men unavailable as a result of their imprisonment as well as unemployment.

Education disparities and joblessness I view as one and the

same, because there is a direct correlation between the two. People who earn an undergraduate degree are projected to earn a million dollars more than a high school dropout over their lifetime. With Black women matriculating from college at a higher rate than Black men and Black men dropping out of high school at a higher rate than Black women, financial compatibility has diminished. If a Black woman is looking for a suitable partner who can at least match her academic achievements and career trajectory, she will be fairly limited.

Dating as far back to the early 1950s, Black families have invested their money in daughters over sons when it comes to post-secondary education. If paying for college wasn't feasible for both, daughters were favored given the greater opportunity for employment for educated Black women. This practice created a natural education gap that has worsened over the years.

Today, the pressure to make money is not the same for Black women, giving them the ability to pursue education over earnings. A beautiful Black woman with a video vixen's waist-to-hip ratio can roll up to the club on her bicycle and still gain attention from Black men. On the other hand, a brotha could look like Boris Kodjoe, but if he pulls up in a Ford Escort, many Black women won't even make eye contact with him. Understanding this dynamic, many Black men place more value on their ability to earn a wage rather than earn a degree.

Statistics show an increasing number of gay Black men is also creating a supply shortage of available Black men for Black women. Gay Black men now make up roughly 3 percent of the total Black male population. A small number, however the effects of gay Black men are far reaching. Per the CDC, among all gay men, Blacks are the most impacted by HIV. "Young Black gay and bisexual men aged 13 to 24 are especially affected by HIV. In 2010 Black men accounted for approximately 4,800 new HIV infections—more than twice as many estimated new infections as young Whites or young Hispanic gay and bisexual men." Bisexual serves as an umbrella to include Black men on the down-low. Whether their homosexual exploitations are open or concealed, it's clear that bisexual Black men are in grave danger of being infected with the HIV virus; especially those living in the southeast, specifically Atlanta. Additionally, some studies have linked fatherless homes to a growing number of young gay men. In essence, gay Black men are negatively impacting marital odds for Black women of their generation as well as the generations to follow.

Quantitatively, these Black male statistics paint a logical picture of how Black women have been negatively impacted by the ever shrinking pool of available Black men. Even within the receding pool lies peril. Considering that many of the remaining good Black men are already taken, what's left is your pick of two poisons; deadbeat Black men or overachieving assholes who think they're God's gift to women.

Young educated Black men have been reading their own press. Overnight they've become macroeconomists. Feeling the lack of competition and strength of a perceived oligopoly, they've driven up the cost of ownership. Like any market with a supply shortage combined with a high demand, many work to maximize their selling power. They view themselves as high commodities, expecting Black women to start bidding wars to win their hearts. Some young women are selling their souls and sacrificing their morals just to get their name in the hat.

37

A Black man in his late twenties (or early thirties) who is single
with a degree, career, car, residence, and no kids views himself as
a rare 20 carat certified VVS diamond. He has internalized all the
rhetoric on the plight of Black women and consciously or subconsciously allowed it to guide his interaction. He keeps his options
open by dating multiple women, convinced that no one is racing to
meet any of them at the altar. He's in no rush to settle, no hurry to
commit. He's only apathetically interested with an ego on par with
Kanye West.

One Friday evening, sitting perched on a barstool at an upscale
sports bar in Hyde Park (Chicago), a Black man turned to me, eyes
suggesting he's somewhere between intoxication and sobriety. His
necktie hanging loosely from his collar signifying it was a long workweek.

"Black women are bitches!"

A bit disturbed but intrigued, I asked, "Why is that?"

He reached for his glass as I sat as stiff as his Vodka, unsure of
which rabbit hole my curiosity might lead me down.

"Ain't no pleasing them!" he said. "I'm 'bout to stick to White
bitches only. They don't give you the same headache."

"I think it's more about the woman than the race." I said, slightly irritated at his dismissive response.

"No. It's Black women. They need to wake up. Black men like
us have plenty options. What Black woman isn't attracted to a successful Black man? They should be happy we even entertaining
them. Your PhD means nothing to me. You know how many wom-
en wish they could be in my inner circle? I got a waiting list."

There was some truth to his words, as callous as they were.
Black women are outpacing all other demographics in matricula-

tion rates. Therefore, their academic successes are viewed less remarkable. An educated Black man carries far more weight than his female equal in the Black community.

A Black man can resemble Eddie the Monster and still get play from many beautiful Black women as long as he's educated and has a career. Why? Because once Black women reach a certain age, typically around their late twenties, they're no longer looking to date "just to date." They are hoping to settle down. No longer looking to be entertained, they want to be crowned. No time for boys. They're in search of their king.

The qualities they want in their king might vary from woman to woman, but one quality that remains consistent across the board is financial stability. The much older pretty-boy thug, who dropped out of high school, yet found a way to pick you up from school every day is not so appealing anymore. Nor is the one-time college football standout, whose NFL career never materialized, yet he is determined to be the remarkably rare 30-year-old rookie.

The Way the Cookie Crumbles

The cumulative effect of the Black male statistics suggests Black women are mere victims of circumstance, damned to single life by forces beyond their control. But are they really?

The mainstream analysis of Black women's wedding bell woes focused exclusively on external stimuli. But keeping the finger pointed at Black men doesn't require any soul searching. What about the less discussed internal Black women issues, the behavioral catalysts that underpin the lack of marriage crisis?

There are a plethora of issues, which all point back to Black women's independence. An independence that has developed through liberalism, freedom of individual, feminism and social equality, not just monetary means. Black America has grown more accepting of the trend-bucking Independent Black Woman to the point of embracing the idea.

The Black church doesn't bat an eye when a mother walks into service with three children and no husband. The public perception of Black female celebrities remains unaffected after accusations of stealing another woman's husband. It's seemingly and increasingly par for the course.

Black women's liberation is not only from Black men, but in some instances fellow Black women and traditional social norms. Black women have assumed a more dominate posture, bullying their way into what they perceive as their rightful place in society as man's unequivocal equal. Moving and shaking like a man, with no time for love, babies, or cooking. And they'll continue until they realize they value family and would prefer the comforting arms of a husband rather than the caress of a complete stranger.

A woman's power, as it relates to man, will always be between her thighs (her cookie). Not because of the unsophisticated nature of woman, but due to the unsophisticated nature of man. Take the kindest, most distinguished gentleman you can think of. Strip him all the way down to his core. What you have left is a man who simply wants to be loved and loved on. You can either reject this reality because it encroaches on your feminism, or you can work to better understand it.

To put it plainly, Black women are losing, attempting to outplay man at his own game rather than work to restore the estranged relationship. There is no benefit to Black women working to be better at being a man rather than becoming a better version of themselves. A woman choosing to take control over her sexuality and explore sex as a sport is not empowering. It's perverting.

Meanwhile, the Black community suffers most from the effects because "two can play the game," but ultimately one race will lose. The result is a subculture of chaos rather than community. The desolate neighborhoods of urban Black America are a sign of the times: trash tossed in the wind, abandoned buildings, and chipped bricks from hollow tips, as we continue to paint the town red with bloodshed.

I wouldn't dare to lump a species as complex as Black women into an all-encompassing category, hurling generalization after generalization at you while ignoring your uniqueness. However, the key imploding issues causing Black women to self-destruct in their pursuit of Black love are interconnected. Rather than discuss the issues as topics, I will explore them in terms of "a woman." She doesn't represent a specific type of Black woman. She is an embodiment of multiple personalities, and un-redeeming qualities. Her legal name is Ms. Independent; however, she has many aliases: Ms. First & Fifteenth, Ms. Transactional, Ms. Promiscuous, Ms. Socialized, Ms. Jackie-Come-Lately, Ms. Build-A-Man, Ms. Bag Lady, and Ms. I-Can-Do-Bad-All-By-Myself. A common denominator in all her code names is "control," aiding in Black America's ongoing social power struggle.

Ms. Independent, the quintessential Mercedes driving, cor-

porate ladder climbing, Type A, competitive forty-year-old corporate executive, spends her weekends sipping mimosas at power
lunches with her posh friends, or jet-setting or being pampered in
some high-end establishment. She's a picture of success, she's not
built to be a housewife. Her off days are spent finding new ways to
toast to the good life. She's living single and loving every minute of
her freedom. Doing everything her way, as master of her kingdom.
She won't be burdened by the stress of a man. She has her credit
card, her girls and her unrivaled sense of fashion.

Suffering slightly from a combination of OCD and carryover
from her managerial corporate responsibilities, Ms. Independent
requires tasks to be done her way, people to march to her beat and
relationships to develop on her time. Such a stringent approach to
life doesn't lend itself to much relationship success. However, she's
content with simply dating on the surface. She's consumed by her
career. It demands most of her focus. Her only interest in a man is
as cuffin' season approaches. There's little a man can provide for
her she can't provide for herself, until she wakes up and she's fifty
without kids or companionship.

Ms. First & Fifteenth is the working-class version of Ms. Independent. Her life is considerably less glamorous, but she's living
fabulous no less, with her knockoff Louis Vuitton handbag. With
three kids and another bun in the oven, she requires assistance from
the government. She's unable to work full-time, yet every Friday
she's dressed to the nines outside her favorite nightclub waiting in
line. She had her first baby when she was only sixteen, forced to
drop out of high school and quit her track team. Robbed of her
youth, made to grow up quickly, the nightclub provides a space
where she can let loose and be kid-free.

She works part-time, so her rent is subsidized. She makes minimum wage, requiring food stamps to feed her babies. She reaches out for help from the government and all her family and friends, too proud to beg for assistance from the men who helped put her in this position.

Ms. Promiscuous, the overly sexual, underdressed, free spirit, who lives her life by the pleasure principles and suffers deeply from hedonism. She's a lone wolf in this sisterhood of divine divas, a rebel willing to sabotage the relationship of her fellow Black sistahs. No boyfriend is safe. No husband is off limits. She's cutthroat, deceitful and emotionally detached. To her, karma is a fragrance she wears proudly on her neck.

In an effort to prove anything men can do she can do better, she has turned what was once said to be a cat-and-mouse game into a cat-and cat game with two predators and no prey. No longer just men using women for sex, but now women using men for sex. No more one-sided one-night stands, waking up to door slams. She's getting dressed and leaving notes on the side of his bed. She uses men and sex to fill an emptiness caused by her father's absence, or to drown the pain from a childhood of molestation. But in this new liberal world void of double standards, she's not hurting she's merely exploring her sexual independence.

Ms. Socialized, she has the right loyalty to the wrong guy. Her thoughts have been compromised by a society that values charisma over character. She passes on the nice guy for someone with a little more swagger. She's infatuated with an image instead of an individual.

She yearns to feel important in the eyes of the world. She wants a man with mass appeal to say "Look at me girls! I got the big catch." The one every girl wanted, but she was lucky enough to get. She basks in her victory until she realizes it's short-lived. The charm that she loves she learns is not exclusive. She transforms into Ms. Bag Lady after losing her man, but you could never lose someone you truly never had.

Ms. Jackie-Come-Lately is often the older sister of Ms. Promiscuous, Ms. Independent or Ms. Socialized. She's had her fun. Her career is established. She's struck out with Mr. Wrong on multiple occasions. She's usually in her late thirties, nervous about her age, fearing if she doesn't find someone soon she won't get her babies. She hates attending weddings, baby showers are even worse. It's just another reminder of her family's generational curse.

She's finding it hard to secure a man, "All the good ones are already taken." She thought time was on her side, but clearly she was mistaken. Now the semi-attractive guy who's been trapped in the friend zone is suddenly more appealing after all her other options have flown.

Ms. Transactional, can be seen every Saturday on a stripper pole, standing on a corner, or as a video vixen shaking her booty in a rap video. She's the type of woman that notices your car before she notices you. She has sex appeal and she knows it, using every inch of her mesmerizing curves to her advantage. Having been reduced to an object, all her money is spent preserving her product.

Like Ms. Promiscuous, Ms. Transactional is highly prone to pregnancy, carelessly playing Russian roulette with her overly sexed body. She's been taught the game by her older female cousin, and proper gold-digger etiquette by her well-seasoned mother. She's not looking for a man. She's looking for a bank account, one with six or seven figures to support her lavish lifestyle.

Ms. Build-a-Man, believes raw potential is all a man needs. Give her a little time, a lot of patience and she can teach any man to lead. She leans toward nurture vs. nature insisting all men are rough around the edges until they've been tailored.

She plays the role of mother more so than mate, constantly grinding and sanding the gritty surface away. She works tirelessly to create her ideal man, but change is something that comes from within. Her pushing only pushes him into the arms of another woman.

Ms. Bag Lady, she's the most abundant and complex. She suffers permanent scars from her disappointing dating past. She's the culmination of all these different Black women prototypes, having made some regrettable mistakes in her previous dating life. She keeps her guard up; ultra-reluctant to trust. She's paralyzed by the idea that someone will cheat on her.

She doesn't go on dates, she goes on interviews. Her time is too precious. Every Black man is guilty until proven innocent. She has many layers of issues for someone to patiently peel back, like Ms. Promiscuous she sometimes suffers from an abusive past. Her scars run deep. She wears her heart on her sleeve, scaring off most men who might have otherwise considered approaching.

Ms. I-Can-Do-Bad-All-By-Myself, at forty-five she's divorced and dead-set on living life by herself. Beyond work and her kids, she has no time for "foolish" men. Her substantial career success came at the cost of her previous marriage. Now she's focused on building her empire, one in which she can play the role of dictator. She's convinced herself that she's better off alone. That's why she chases off any man who challenges her throne. Though she denies it, she's slightly bitter at the opposite sex. It's evident in the way she preaches to her son about respect. It's not as much about his actions as it is his look, she stares at him and sees a familiar love crook. He's the spitting image of his father's face, a constant reminder of her darker days.

When we look at these types we see that with increased independence, Black women find themselves in an ironic place. They are victims of a cliché, as it appears that they've "cut off one's nose to spite one's face." It's not as if Black women have divorced the idea of marriage. I've attended enough Black wedding receptions and witnessed the ruthless pursuit of even a symbol of good fortune, as Black women nearly bludgeoned each other to catch the bouquet, to know the idea of marriage is still alive and well.

There are many Black women who dream of the day their father can walk them down the aisle. The problem with this fantasy is there's often no father to escort the bride and the bride herself is unprepared to live out her wedding vows.

For women, marriage (and motherhood) requires submission and a healthy dose of sacrifice. In this new era of jet-setting, fashion-forward, boss lady, Independent Black Women, many are unwilling to play second fiddle to their spouse. They have their own goals and aspirations that extend far beyond a crock pot and the kitchen. However, they will learn that sacrifice comes with the territory.

Independent Black Women love a Black man with power, no matter how much power she has individually. You will never see a powerful Black woman with a weak Black man. Power seeks power and iron sharpens iron. Therefore, the potential for a power struggle will never be fully eliminated; it is only mitigated through a healthier understanding of life and relationships.

Look no further than America's former First Family for an example. A graduate of Princeton University and Harvard Law School, First Lady Michelle Obama is a phenomenal woman in her own right, with the capacity to one day become Commander-In-Chief of this nation. She's added many titles to her name over the years: lawyer, writer, public servant, role model. But first and foremost she is a wife and a mother. She understands and embraces this distinction better than most "lady bosses."

President Obama explains in *The Audacity of Hope* the challenging dynamic of his and Michelle's relationship prior to his presidency as he pursued a career in politics.

It was only upon reflection, after the trials of those years had passed and the kids had started school, that I began to appreciate what Michelle had been going through at the time, the struggles so typical of today's working mothers. For no matter how liberated I liked to see myself as—no matter how much I told myself that Michelle and I were equal partners, and that her dreams and ambitions were as important as my own—the fact was that when children showed up, it was Michelle and not I who was expected to make the necessary adjustments. … she was the one who had to put her career on hold. She was the one who had to make sure that the kids were fed and bathed every night.

As a result of Michelle's sacrifice, the Obama family is collectively in a better position. Barack is concluding a successful two terms, Malia is headed to Harvard, Sasha is thriving, and Michelle, if she so desires, is in a perfect situation to make a future run for President. Clearly, sacrifice doesn't require you to *sacrifice* your dreams.

At the end of the day, you have to keep life in perspective. Constantly ask yourself "What's most important to me?" If you desire to get married and have a family, accept the fact that, whether your husband is running for president or working the third shift at a power plant, you will likely be required to pick up the slack at home—whether you are a lawyer or a school teacher.

Most men enjoy working. We thrive off the pursuit of something greater...and always something greater. I've yet to meet the man who doesn't plan to take over the world. Men are natural conquerors. It's what gives our life purpose. Our purpose is fulfilled through our quest for wealth and reverence. However, purpose alone does not sustain us. We need our life to have meaning. Meaning comes from having a family and leaving a legacy, and being a provider. Purpose and meaning combined completes us. This paradigm alone is why most men get married. The sooner Black women understand this the better they will be able to navigate through the landscape of this male dominated world without feeling underappreciated and marginalized by their spouses, or worse husbandless and in competition with every man she meets.

THE INFLUENCE

INFLUENCE [inflŏŏəns]: the capacity or power of persons or things to be a compelling force on or produce effects on the actions, behavior, opinions, etc., of others

With an estimated 67 percent of Black children currently being raised in a household where the father is absent, much of the issues related to Black women's independence stems from upbringing for the younger generations. Proper modeling of a healthy family unit has never been a part of their experience. They've only been privy to the matriarchal world of a single mother, where women bring home the bacon, fry it in a pan, then take out any garbage left over from breakfast.

Even before we can talk we can absorb sound and images. From birth, as our hearing strengthens and vision comes into focus, we are subjected to the world around us. These sounds and images help shape our perspective and become the lens through which we view the rest of life. Because what the eyes see and the ears hear, the mind believes, even if it's a distortion of reality.

We are all products of our environment. That is a fact, but there are certain characteristics of a person that are innate. For instance, if you were raised by wolves, you would act like a wolf. All the cultural elements of wolves would be reflected in your behavior. On the other hand, if you were raised by monkeys, your behavior would reflect the monkeys' way of life. These are all learned behaviors that can fluctuate from culture to culture. The characteristics of you that remain consistent, whether being raised by monkeys

51

or wolves, are the true essence of you as a person. These traits are independent of all environmental influences. Now replace wolves and monkeys with single-parent households and double-parent households and the dynamic remains true. With so many Black women being born to single-mothers their entire way of thinking and approach to life has been distorted. Out of necessity they've had to learn to be independent as a part of their coming of age—*learn* being the operative word. These behaviors don't represent the true essence of Black women. It's simply a conditioned behavior created for self-preservation.

As a single Black mother preparing your daughter for the world, you would be negligent not to teach her how to survive on her own. This is in turn creating a younger generation of aggressive, Type A, Black women with traditionally masculine tendencies (and a growing number of young Black men who display hypermasculinity or feminine tendencies). The ideals of independence become so engrained in the fabric of the person that cultivating a healthy relationship is impossible without changing habits. Sometimes change is less about becoming someone different and more about finding your true identity. Who am I really? Why do I think the way I think? Why do I dress the way I dress? Why do I talk the way I talk? Why do I desire the things—shoes, clothes, jewelry, cars—I desire?

Beyond our immediate environment, much of our influence comes in the form of popular culture. For Black folk roughly forty and under that denotes hip hop culture. Arguably succeeding the Black Power Movement in size and scope, the Hip Hop Movement and subsequent leaders have indeed set the course for Black America over the past three decades. There are no more Hueys, Stokelys, or Angelas, only Beys, Yeezys and Hovas.

When the Black Power Movement first launched in the sixties, it had a profound transformative effect on Black culture that remained unrivaled until the rise of the Hip Hop Movement. From music to fashion, attitude and language, the Black Power Movement ushered us into a new era of Blackness that was bold and conscious. Music became more racially and politically charged. Black men and women began wearing their hair natural ushering in the age of the "afro." The term "soul brotha" and "soul sistah" became popular when greeting each other. Black southern cuisine became "soul food." All of this branding served as a way to unify Black Americans and encourage us to reject Eurocentric societal influences.

Hip hop culture has had the same, perhaps stronger, effect on today's Black culture, influencing all facets of everyday Black life: music, fashion, art and language, but also delving deeper into the psyche of Black people influencing their attitudes and values, dictating what is important and what is irrelevant.

From the outset, hip hop music functioned as a loudspeaker to amplify the struggles and racial inequalities of disenfranchised and marginalized urban Black communities. It was self-expression personified. Hip hop music was able to successfully integrate lower-class Black culture into the mainstream media and make it relevant. This caused a fundamental shift in beliefs. Instead of lower-class Blacks feeling like they had to conform to the world, hip hop music brought the rest of the world to the hood. It made lower-class Blacks feel comfortable being themselves.

At some point it became more about making money than making a statement. Major record labels began signing rap artists to lucrative record deals and with that hip hop went from being an

53

underground genre of music to the top of the Billboard charts. What started as a movement predominately for young Black men spread to all types of young demographics.

Above and beyond the smooth beats and catchy choruses, the broader American infatuation with rap is due to the cocky, brass, flamboyant nature of the music. If you are a shy person, it helps you take on the persona of someone who is confident. If you're already confident, it makes you obnoxiously arrogant.

Hip hop music possesses the power to bring people of all races together under one roof to move to one beat, creating the type of unity and dream Dr. King preached about, fifty-three years ago, on the steps of the Lincoln Memorial. However, the problem with the picture becomes obvious once you introduce the audio.

Hip hop music, and the culture it created, is the epitome of life imitating *imitation* art. Less than half of what's portrayed is real. The glorification of violence, misogyny, drugs and consumerism in the lyrics are hardly King-esque. Rappers represent a faction of Black Americans with a "win by any means necessary" mentality, and no regard for social responsibility.

But, we all play a part in preserving the integrity of our community. In order to do so you must be willing to challenge the status quo. You must abandon what you have casually accepted as music and seek true artistry. In a Black male dominated industry, the majority of rap lyrics are misogynistic, yet Black women rap right along ignoring the message.

The music attempts to reduce women's bodies to sex objects existing only for male satisfaction. With Black women being equal consumers of the content, they are conditioned to respond favorably to sexual advances. Jay-Z's infamous line in the song "Best of

Me" literally helped seal the deal on multiple occasions throughout my college career—I'm sure I wasn't alone. "That's high school, making me chase you 'round for months. Have an affair. Act like an adult for once."

Much of the content highlights Black male rappers as dominant figures with the cash and charisma (swagger) to have any woman they choose—validated by the half-dozen half-naked women vying for a position next to them in the music video.

Black women struggle to make it in the industry. The few who succeed—Lil' Kim being the most infamous—understand how to successfully balance the power. Since most rap songs paint women as sex objects, they use the same dynamic in reverse to their advantage.

If your dude come close to me
He gon' wanna ride off in ghost [Rolls-Royce] with me
I might let your boy chauffeur me
But he gotta eat the booty like groceries

Or

When he fuck me good I take his ass to Red Lobster,
Cause I slay
When he fuck me good I take his ass to Red Lobster,
Cause I slay
If he hit it right, I might take him on a flight on my chopper,
Cause I slay
Drop him off at the mall, let him buy some J's, let him shop up,
Cause I slay

Vulgar language aside, these lyrics are pure lies. What's clearly ficti-
tious is the notion that a woman with the type of money and power
to afford a helicopter would ever entertain a man she would need
to "take" to Red Lobster. Last I checked an average entrée at Red
Lobster will set you back about twenty dollars. If he doesn't have at
least forty dollars to cover both meals, it's highly doubtful he even
exists in her world.

It's all an image, instead of being the prey female rappers (and
singers) use their status as power over men to lure them into sexual
favors. They become predators and men become their prey, creating a false dichotomy that places Black men and women in the
position of either hunter or game. Black men can either choose
to prey on Black women, or have Black women prey on them and
vice versa, perpetuating a cycle of distrust and stirring the pot of
dysfunction. The result is a group of individuals so paranoid about
being played that they keep everyone at arm's length. Black men
treat Black women like they're a dime-a-dozen and Black wom-
en act nonchalant about Black men—neither side willing to allow
themselves to be vulnerable.

The consistent rhetoric from Black male rappers is anti-wom-
an and anti-marriage. With female artists now emulating the men,
producing discourse that is anti-marriage and anti-man, we've
reached a place of self-hate that is collectively anti-Black and wholly destructive.

Rap's foundation is built on image and possessions. The image
controls perception and perception creates the reality. Essentially
we've swallowed the blue pill and entered into the matrix, a perpetual state of illusion and subliminal seduction where the fantasy world feels more real and reality is a less desirable lifestyle. We

operate in a space where women who cover up are considered old fashioned, and men who adore and respect women are labeled as swag-less. Words like "bitch" have morphed into a term of endearment used by Black men and Black women alike.

Around every major city on any given Friday or Saturday night there are thousands of people attempting to live out their own rap video; men pulling up in Mercedes, Lexuses and Bentleys, picking ladies out of the crowd to join them in the VIP room; women dressed to impress with their finest weaves and a face full of makeup standing at the front door of the night club expecting the VIP treatment. These are not all women of the night or gold diggers looking for a "come up." Sprinkled in are professional women with multiple degrees and six-figure salaries subjecting themselves to such unflattering behavior. Why? Because it's not about money, it's about perceived status and wanting to feel important according to an artificial and dangerous social construct. Where is Vaughn "Dap" Dunlap to yell "Wake up!"?

Ms. Independent Feminist

Prior to the hip hop generation, Black woman's desire for independence, was largely influenced by the Black Feminist Movement. Since slavery, Black people have fought to renounce the second-class citizenship bestowed upon them by the White race. In the face of imminent danger we fearlessly marched through the valley of the shadow of death time after time, trusting God would see us through to the other side. Some made it. Others perished. Many who died at the hands of evil accomplished more in death than they ever could in life. The African American race is further along the equality continuum as a result of their ultimate sacrifice.

If not for resistance maybe our current social position would be a mirror image of slavery—modern day. One could make the argument that America is still operating within that framework, as many Blacks remain chained to the bottom of America's capitalistic economy, working as laborers with wages that after rent, utilities, and groceries leaves them broke and slaves to poverty. That's debatable. However, what's undeniable is wherever Black people rank in American society, Black women are a few steps behind.

In terms of equal rights, Black women have always been lowest on the totem pole. An esoteric truth that routinely escapes most Civil Rights storytelling is that the Black Feminist Movement was born out of the internal fight for Black women to find their voice within the Civil Rights struggle. Many Black women perceived the Civil Rights Movement as a fight for equality for all Black *men* not all Black *people*.

At the same time, a second wave of the Feminist Movement (or Women's Movement) was growing in power—a practical effort to address issues of women's rights. Black women found themselves in a tug of war to determine what was most paramount, issues of race or issues of gender. The answer was "both." Being born a Black woman meant learning how to achieve success with two strikes against you—Black and female.

It is largely believed that racial discrimination within the Feminist Movement and gender discrimination within the Civil Rights Movement left Black women yearning for a political movement of their own—one more germane to their unique struggle. This desire

culminated in the launch of the National Black Feminist Organization (NBFO) in 1973.

At its core, the movement aimed to bring awareness and reso-
lution to the interconnected inequalities of race and gender facing
women of color—a group who felt little value was placed upon
them in America's White-male dominated society. Atop the list was
the age-old struggle against sexual violence. Black Feminists' an-
ti-rape activism exposed the darker side of the Civil Rights era that
too often left Black women gang raped, beaten and killed at the
hands of White men. Like dogs marking their territory, rape was
used to remind Black men and Black boys alike that White men
controlled their communities. The inability of Black men to protect
their women resulted in a psychological castration, which precipi-
tated sexual violence within the Black community.

Black women came under attack by the very men intended to
protect them. Even worse, Black women were forced to remain
emotionless while being violated. They were also required to suffer
in silence afraid to demonize Black men in a society that already
viewed them as threats, unwilling to subject them to a justice system
out to genocide Black men. Eldridge Cleaver, a self-identified rapist
and former member of the Black Panther Party leadership—now
deceased—wrote in his 1968 book *Soul on Ice*:

> I started out practicing [rape] on Black girls in the ghetto— in the
> Black ghetto where dark and vicious deeds appear not as aberra-
> tions or deviations from the norm, but as part of the sufficiency of
> the Evil of a day—and when I considered myself smooth enough,
> I crossed the tracks and sought out white prey. I did this consciously,
> deliberately, willfully, methodically.

The NBFO also aimed to empower Black women by redefining their traditional roles by way of eliminating stereotypes, creating a sisterhood and establishing a political agenda specific to Black women's issues. Much like the Black Power Movement, the Black Feminist Movement's success can't be quantified by the amount of NBFO members or the sum of political victories. The movement can only be measured in terms of lumens due to its illuminating power. The movement encouraged Black women to dare greatly at a time in American history when being a Black woman meant staying in your place, a seemingly innocuous feat if not for the fact that Black women had no place in society. Prior to 1950, Black women were largely absent from the public. A Black woman's presence was mainly at home as a homemaker or in someone else's home as the hired help.

During the movement, a new ideology was birthed, a belief that ignited Black women in a way that had never been seen before. It forever changed the way Black women viewed themselves. The Black Feminist Movement symbolized beauty, dignity and power; the beauty of a Black woman, the dignity of self-worth and the power to overcome injustice. Through the Black Feminist Movement, women were able to find their voice. Instead of feeling stifled by a male-dominated Civil Rights Movement, Black women gave voice to their struggle. There was a renewed sense of self-worth and pride among Black women that had been lost over hundreds of years of slavery and the aftermath. Being a Black woman no longer brought about a feeling of despair; it was an honor and privilege. It qualified you as a member of the Black Feminist Movement.

Not all positives came out of the Black Feminist Movement, however. Some viewed the movement as divisive, because it promoted separatism within the greater Civil Rights Movement; but one would be hard-pressed to argue that it didn't fundamentally change the nation's perception of Black women and their perception of self. The movement was by no means an attempt by Black Women to sabotage Black men; many remained steadfast in their support of the Civil Rights Movement. The Black Feminist Movement was Black women controlling what was within their power, creating a platform to call attention to their unique issues.

To deny the impact of the Black Feminist Movement is to subscribe to the counterintuitive belief that White men would voluntarily surrender a seat at the corporate roundtable to a Black woman. *Nothing* has been given to Black women. They've had to constantly fight through barriers to find success, earning every inch of prosperity achieved. The foundation of their makeup is rooted deeply in persistence and long-suffering. There would be no Oprah Winfrey if not for the audacity to believe Black women deserved a presence in daytime television. But before Oprah there was Angela... Audre... Florynce... and countless other pioneers.

Without question our society has reaped endless benefits from progressive Black women. These fierce ladies have served as habitual challengers of the status quo. They've championed many causes and provided much intellectual capital, advancing women's rights and civil rights while defeating negative stereotypes. However, as the pendulum swings breaking through barriers for Black women, it has doubled as a wrecking ball in the opposite direction. The Black community has felt the acute adverse effects from the demolition. Where Black women have gained ground financially and politically, the Black community has lost ground socially. To conveniently ignore the obvious oppositional effects the Black Feminist

Movement has had on Black family dynamics would be unilateral and irresponsible.

Many believe the peak in divorce rates in the seventies and eighties was an anomaly largely triggered by the second wave of the Feminist Movement—a chain reaction caused by women's liberation. Women file for divorce twice as often as men. Therefore, when experiencing rising divorce rates, it's a direct reflection of a rise in women's expectations. As a microcosm of the larger movement, the Black Feminist Movement caused social and economic turmoil. Black women entering the workforce altered gender roles. They were no longer in search of a breadwinner husband. They desired to earn their own living and husbands who respected them as equals.

Today, Black feminist thought remains widespread throughout the Black community. The combined feeling of sexual-racial oppression extends beyond a title or a movement into the stifled private thoughts of most Black women. Many of whom are not "officially" associated with the Black Feminist Movement but identify, in part or wholly, with the ideology. These beliefs serve as the catalyst for Black women's independence, declaring war against the sexual oppression by Black men and subsequently driving a wedge between Black men and women in the process.

These polarizing beliefs even create competition among spouses. Young Black married professionals arguing over whose career is more important, both jockeying for more time to devote to their goals and more support at home. As newlyweds, you might be able to sneak by, at the risk of quality time, with both pursing their goals full throttle; however, the moment you introduce children that model is broken. Divorce court is full of professional women not willing to relinquish their high corporate positions to provide more support at home. They would rather stand alone than lose ground.

As a result, many extreme Black feminists have chosen the path of lesbianism. In 1974, an entire organization of lesbian Black Feminists was created under the name The Combahee River Collective. Their strong opinions on the roles of Black women didn't lend themselves to heterosexual relationships. Their political views were so one-sided only another Black [feminist] woman could possibly embrace them.

To every issue there is a starting point. Understanding history helps us put Black relationship dynamics in context. So when we discuss the 21st century Independent Black Woman, we must acknowledge that this longing for independence and competition between Black men and women is by no means a new phenomenon. Black feminists have clamored for liberation from the "oppressive" Black man for half a century, ushering us through this slow fade.

New-Age Black Feminism

With the turn of the millennium, primitive feminist beliefs have been usurped by New-Age Black feminist theories, submerged in self-objectification. Black women objectify themselves as well as other Black women. No more present is this paradigm than in Black gentleman's clubs. The explosion of women patronage is the personification of New-Age Black feminism. Naked female dancers shaking and working the poles while female patrons flock to the stage makin' it rain on 'em. Many of them are heterosexual, which begs the question "What do they gain from the experience?"

Due to the glorification in rap music, strip clubs in the Black community have become as much of a status symbol as it is a pleasure bastion. In a game of "Who can blow the most money in a strip club?" Black boss ladies want a piece of the action. Instead of creating their own pinnacles of success, Black women have piggybacked on Black men's idea of success. Out to prove to Black men they have the same earning muscle, degrading other women makes them feel empowered. Their mentality is that I could be in here shaking my ass for cash too; instead I'm throwing money at you because I'm a boss.

New-Age feminism intensifies the us-against-them dichotomy. To the degree that even when being degraded Black strippers are celebrating the success of other Black women while embracing their own independence. The New-Age motto is, "Don't let men objectify you; objectify yourself!" It suggests women use their sexuality for power and personal gain. Far from an ode to their ancestry, their brand of feminism doesn't represent the true spirit of Black femininity. New-Age Black feminist thought, on the surface, seems more like convenient feminism than empowerment—picking and choosing when to promote healthy female imagery or bombard us with hyper-sexualized alter egos. Scroll through Instagram for five minutes. The amount of Black women baring their bodies for a like and a following is at an all-time high.

Previously, Black feminism endeavored to redefine gender roles. Today, Black feminism is about eliminating gender roles altogether. Earlier Black feminists were deliberate about the image they projected. Desiring to be respected as leaders and independent thinkers, they safeguarded their appearance to ensure it reflected the level of reverence they sought. New-Age Black feminism is unconcerned with respect. It's about eliminating double standards and stereotypes, giving Black women the freedom to "act like a man" without being labeled a "whore" or a "tramp." This feminist-led No Shame Movement flies in the face of traditional Christian beliefs about sexuality.

Essentially, no shaming is a license to live recklessly. The endgame is a society where women give each other high fives for sleeping with a man on the first night, turning the proverbial "walk of shame" into the "walk of fame." However, there is nothing liberating about promiscuity or a sexually transmitted disease. New-Age feminists are seeking a society without shame and judgment. They seem to revel in a society that is devoid of responsibility for our actions and doesn't consider its ramifications, or what we are teaching our children.

Rather than expend energy on real social and political issues impacting Black women—from disparities in medical research, diagnosis and treatment of diseases, to hurdles in education, to a gender-centric salary gap that increases with the introduction of race—many New-Age Black feminists seem more interested in a "penis" measuring competition.

The obvious objection to this New-Age ideology is that the Black Feminist Movement was created in part due to sexism: prejudice, stereotyping, and discrimination within the Civil Rights Movement. Feminism is cerebral not sexual. Black feminists refused to be relegated to objects, only performing roles deemed appropriate for women. They relied on their Black girl magic: strength, intelligence, talent and work ethic to remove the glass ceiling—not their bodies. Thus, objectifying yourself makes you a Black feminist

65

as much as walking on all fours makes you human. The two go together like oil and water.

I consider myself a feminist. I believe in social, political and economic equality for all women and stand against sexual violence and double standards. However, my support of women's rights ends where human rights begins. Where women's rights become destructive infringing upon a fetus' right to live, or when women's rights create a false narrative that begs the question "Do I join the No Shame Movement and sleep around to prove I'm progressive or do I remain traditional and brainwashed by society's patriarchal influence?" Surely, there are many modern Black women who carry the torch of the Black feminists of yesteryear; however, this New-Age feminist belief is the more pervasive philosophy in mainstream society.

*D'*evils: *D*ivorce and the *D*evaluing of Marriage

There is an old saying "If you tell a lie big enough and keep repeating it, people will eventually come to believe it." The myth that 50 percent of marriages are ending in divorce has been that big lie repeated ad nauseam. Truth is 50 percent of marriages haven't ended in divorce since Lionel Richie left the Commodores. Divorce statistics reached a critical mass in the seventies and early eighties, but has been on the decline for the past three decades. Marrying later and for love is thought to be the cause for the decline.

Current statistics suggest that two-thirds of marriages beginning in the nineties or later will go the distance. Yet for some reason we can't seem to shake the stigma of our distant past. It's like the grade school bully, who is now a responsible adult, being viewed through the lens of his childhood playground cruelty. The rumors of marital demise have been flagrantly exaggerated. However, the rumors have proven to be an effective fear tactic as marriage rates are at an all-time low. The increased social acceptance of single mothers and shacking up couples notwithstanding, there is a large number of people terrified of marriage.

If commercial aircrafts were believed to have a failure rate of 50 percent, it's unlikely that air travel would be a popular means of mass transportation. Perception is reality. Marriage is no different. These false marital statistics have deterred many young couples from even beginning the journey.

Indeed, it is a commitment that should be taken seriously and given due diligence; however, marriage is nothing to fear. Will there be scary moments? Absolutely! If a couple has been married for some length of time, their relationship has likely run the gamut of emotions from extreme highs full of joy and satisfaction, to extreme lows plagued with disappointment and frustration. Marriage is one of the toughest challenges you will ever accept in life. It's also one of the most rewarding.

There are many great aspects of a good marriage; best of all is that you have someone significant to walk through life with. The amount of joy and balance my wife, Leanne, has brought to my life is immeasurable. Her essence alone makes me want to be a better person. She is beautiful—inside and out, through and through. Her style and grace is so becoming. She's always respectful, always ladylike, never sacrificing her beliefs or jeopardizing her integrity. She never attempts to be anything more than what God has already made her...wonderful! She is a constant breath of fresh air. No matter how rough my day is going, her warm embrace can help change everything. However, even two people who love and adore each other will struggle to agree in marriage because, more often than not, opposites attract.

What makes marriage so difficult is also what makes it so fulfilling; it's until death do you part. Five years in, you could still be in marital bliss. Ten years in, you could be ready to call it quits. A marriage has to evolve to last. The people, and by virtue the marriage, have to be dynamic. The marriage will constantly change over time. It will be tested by living together, having children, not having children, starting a career, changing careers, deaths in the family, relocations and family investments. These changes will either put a strain on the marriage or further cement it. If you weather each storm together, the bond becomes so strong that even a tornado won't be able to break it.

Leanne and I have been through our rounds of battles. We've wondered if we made the wrong decision and if our marriage would make it, all the while, feeling guilty about questioning whether or not we *wanted* the marriage to make it. We both have a healthy respect for each other's ability to walk away from this union. At the end of the day, how we've reached nine years is our commitment to each other. A commitment that says no matter what, I will not give up. A commitment that says in the face of intense turmoil I will not turn my back on you. I'm committed to this love boat whether we're coasting along smoothly or faced with tumultuous seas.

We don't subscribe to a Hollywood image of love. Hollywood teaches us to leave if you're unhappy. God teaches us that love is a choice not a feeling. In love you feel every emotion. Throughout it all, you choose to celebrate the good in your spouse. When quitting is truly not an option, you will find a way to restore your relationship. Obviously, there are certain transgressions that can push a marriage beyond the point of reconciliation, but you'd be amazed at what a couple can overcome in marriage when divorce is removed as a safeguard.

When people ask me how long I've been married, I've always answered using "strong" as my affix: three years strong, five years strong, seven years strong or nine years strong. How can I refer to my marriage as "strong" if it's been afflicted with challenges? Easy. We're still married. Many marriages don't make it to year one, let alone year three, five, or seven. If you've experienced longevity it's not by accident, it's by choice.

"Army Strong" is a popular slogan of the United States Army. What makes an army strong is the strength of its soldiers' commitment, not physical strength. It is strength of purpose, strength of character, an emotional strength, a strength to endure. With the odds stacked against them and wounded soldiers among them, this band of brothers all yell "Hooah!" and keep fighting until there are no more bad guys standing or no more breath in their bodies.

When I reflect on marriage as a whole, I picture a battlefield. I see a man and a woman pinned down in a bunker, standing back-to-back, taking fire. Both war-ready with face paint and AK-47 assault rifles clinched within their grips. They're prepared to protect against enemies from all sides. He has to trust she will protect his blindside. She has to trust he'll do the same. Both have to be willing to sacrifice their own lives to save the other. It's the only way they survive. The moment trust becomes compromised and you start to question whether your partner is an enemy or a friendly, you turn on each other. The consequence is friendly fire.

Friendly fire doesn't exist in a healthy marriage. It can only happen if the two begin to separate and turn on each other. As long as the relationship stays intact with both partners standing back-to-back, it is impossible. In love, just as in life, nothing is promised. Before you say "I do" and commit to spending the rest of your life with someone, make sure you are prepared to lay down your life for them. Make sure you're marrying a fighter, someone who won't wave the white flag at the first sign of adversity. Make sure you have the basic training you need to fight off the enemy. There will be many.

When highlighting the fact that Black marriages occurred at a higher rate in the fifties and sixties than today, I'm typically met with a rebuttal suggesting that Black women are now putting their careers first and that twentieth century Black women only married because they felt trapped by social norms, and sought financial stability due to the lack of opportunity for Black women in the workforce. All valid points; however, beyond these enablers, Black women married because they had a twentieth century view of marriage.

A twentieth century Black woman approached marriage like she approached her job. People didn't bounce around from company to company looking for greater upward mobility. Work, like marriage, was a commitment and duty; much like serving your country. You wore it proudly like a badge of honor.

There are a multitude of reasons why marriages die, ranging from death by a thousand cuts to a single dagger to the heart. However, there are common themes surrounding divorce that pinpoint frequent problems. The most abundant is motive. Many marriages are doomed even before they begin because one or both spouses enter marriage for all the wrong reasons.

For many Black women, marriage provides financial security. For them, marrying into money is more important than love or compatibility. The idea reads well on paper, but living it out is another matter entirely. There are many books and articles written by women advocating other women to marry for money. Finances should definitely be evaluated when considering a life partner, but marrying solely for money is never a good choice. Money won't bring you happiness if you are an unhappy person. Unhappy people find ways to remain unhappy regardless of the circumstances.

Marrying for money will only give a man power over you. The concept of Black women marrying for money is an old practice that has long existed in many cultures. The history of bride price, or a dowry of money or goods given to the family of a bride by the bridegroom or his family, can be traced back to early African civilization. Love was absent from the equation. Bride and groom were typically strangers to one another. Marriage was strictly a business arrangement.

Fast forward to the early 1900s, women married for money because they weren't allowed to join the workforce. Besides her negligible odd jobs, she could only rely on her husband to earn a living decent enough to support the family. Thus, Black parents encouraged their daughters to "marry well." With not much capital available to Black people, marrying well in that time period could be the difference between having food to eat or going to bed hungry. Today, Black women are thriving financially. The paradigm has shifted; still many Black women are in search of a man with money, not to provide for them but to match their earning potential.

Some women are seeking validation through marriage. Society has conditioned women to believe being chosen in marriage affirms them, "If you liked it then you shoulda put a ring on it!" It becomes a competition. When women are in their early twenties they compete for success, who can finish their undergraduate and graduate degrees first, or who can land that lucrative post-grad career. Once they reach their late twenties success takes on a different shape; one that looks like a diamond. All your friends begin to jump the broom, you find yourself lined up on a wall, akin to a childhood pick-up game of dodgeball; you want nothing more than to be chosen first. Even in a childhood game of dodgeball being picked meant you had value. You were a winner. You brought something to the table that others recognized and wanted. The last person standing was the least valued, the kid chosen by default when all other options were exhausted.

Children can also be a strong motive for marriage. While I'm a strong advocate for a traditional family structure, I don't believe sharing a child is grounds for tying the knot. Children alone cannot sustain a marriage if other key ingredients are absent. There has to be shared spiritual beliefs, an open line of communication and a heavy dose of humility and selflessness. Unfortunately, in this day and age some parents are virtually strangers to each other. The kid came as a consequence of a few nights of unprotected passion or a casual relationship with no substance. You would do your kid and yourself a favor by not committing to someone you barely know. The aftermath of these situations is generally worse for the child. A union lacking in strong marital traits will create an environment that is not conducive to positive growth in a child.

To a far greater extent than women, men place a tremendous

amount of stock on physical appearance, so much that some men are willing to ignore obvious signs of incompatibility just to wake up to a pretty face every morning. And there are plenty of women willing to play the role of trophy wife. The problem with this scenario is, if it took looks to get him it will take looks to keep him. Unfortunately, there's this thing called "gravity" that will cause areas to sag over time. Beauty will fade. That is a certainty. What's uncertain is a man's commitment when his professed love is based on looks. After you're past your prime, he may develop a wandering eye that leads him to the arms of a younger and tighter version of you.

Pressure from peers and parents alike has proven to be the tipping point for some women who have taken a leap of faith without measuring the trajectory. It forces you to take a chance on a man who falls well below your physical, spiritual or financial threshold. You then find yourself constantly yearning for him to improve, but he can't yield results beyond his capacity. He feels unappreciated. You feel unfulfilled. The combination of the two can lead both spouses to stray. Then divorce becomes inevitable.

If a marriage was built on a faulty foundation, it will reveal itself when put through a stress test. Life's unforeseen challenges will place tremendous amounts of pressure on a marriage to measure its strength. When put to the test, the weakest areas of the marriage will collapse first. If they are not addressed and strengthened, the entire marriage will fold. Once you reinforce all the areas, life has its way of applying more pressure, forcing the new weakest areas to succumb to the stress. Over the years, you will have to constantly step through the strengthening process—over and over again.

For Leanne and I, each child brought about a new and different challenge to our relationship, forcing us to reinforce areas of our marriage that were vulnerable. To still be married after three kids is a testament to the strength of our marriage.

Statistics suggest that couples who marry later in life have a lower divorce rate. I'm convinced these couples are more successful because generally there are no young kids in the equation. I honestly can't remember having an argument before children. I'm sure they occurred, but they were few and far between. As newlyweds little changed about our relationship dynamic besides intimacy and living together. For some living together can be a feat in and of itself. However, our transition produced minimal conflict, with the exception of the tug-of-war over the toilet roll.

Growing up, my family always put the roll on the holder with the tissue dispensing underneath the roll. Leanne grew up putting the roll on the holder with the tissue dispensing over the top. She tried to convert me, but I resisted! I would go behind her and change the rolls on the holder when she wasn't paying attention. Eventually, I gave in and we decided to use her over-the-top tissue loading method (I bet you never knew loading toilet tissue was so scientific). It's been almost nine years since she converted me to the OTT tissue method. I'm fully transformed. Now, whenever I cross paths with underneath dispensing it seems foreign to me.

Other than that slight power struggle and a few others, we navigated well through our new living arrangement and newlywed stage. Sometimes I gave in. Sometimes she did. Other times, we compromised. It was a new day when our daughter, Zoe, arrived. A rude awakening realizing we couldn't continue to come and go as we pleased. There was this new concept called "scheduling." I would break out in hives every time I tried it. I was used to us going to work and meeting up for lunch regularly. After work, we would spend the rest of the evening as we saw fit. At times that meant coming together for an activity: dinner, movie, workout, church or flying solo and reconvening later at our condo. It was common for me to hit the gym for three hours after work. I played basketball and worked out without considering the time other than being conscious of the gym closing.

Having a child forced unwanted structure into our leisure time. Being parents meant accounting for 24/7 coverage for our child. "Who's gonna watch the baby?" became a frequent game we would play around the house, proceeded by an intense game of Rock-Paper-Scissors to determine the outcome. Even though my family was from Chicago, we didn't have a strong support system. My mother still worked and my sister had work and my niece to keep her busy.

Leanne was from Southern California. She moved to Chicago with her parents after high school. A career change required her dad to move to the Midwest. By the time Zoe arrived he had semi-retired and her parents were back living in a warmer climate.

We didn't have many options if we needed a collective break. This was further compounded by a serious case of acid reflux that caused Zoe to have several choking episodes, the earliest at only seven-weeks old.

During these episodes—being too young to spit or even turn her head—she would suffer from a deadly buildup of mucous. My baby girl would lie there gasping and gagging until we suctioned her. I would lay her on her side in my lap and stick the bulb syringe in the back of her mouth near the bottom of her cheek and suction repeatedly while she screamed hysterically.

It was dangerous for her, and all the more scary for us because the pediatrician warned that if we inserted the bulb tip too deep we could cause a bronchial spasm, narrowing her airway even more. We would try not to panic watching our precious baby struggle to breathe, but once screams turned silent we knew the situation was rapidly deteriorating.

During the worst episode, we had to call the paramedics who quickly determined she needed more invasive attention. We were asked to bring her down to the ambulance for further treatment. I lay on the gurney holding Zoe, while Leanne sat motionless across from me paralyzed by her emotions. The paramedic took a long thin tube and fished it from Zoe's nose down into her throat. Then, he flipped a switch and suctioned out all the content from her esophagus. She could finally breathe clearly again. So exhausted from the ordeal she fell immediately asleep. It's an experience she won't remember, but we will never forget.

Needless to say we didn't feel safe leaving our baby with any-one who didn't feel comfortable with her condition or understand the onset of it. That left mommy and daddy to provide 99 percent of the caregiving, with Leanne providing the majority as now a full-time stay-at-home mother. We went roughly a year and a half without a date post-baby. Our situation necessitated that we often had to divide and conquer to get tasks accomplished. For instance, one person went grocery shopping while the other gave the baby a bath.

Absences became more apparent. If one of us was indulging in a leisurely activity it left the other to pick up the slack at home. My three-hour gym sessions now meant, "I was being inconsiderate." They would soon die a slow death along with other time-consum-ing hobbies. Workouts were now relegated to early mornings or late at night so they didn't interfere with family time.

Parenthood forced our focus off of each other. Zoe became the center of attention. Most of our communication revolved around her in some fashion. She was everything we prayed for and more in a daughter. Her bold personality kept us entertained every moment she was awake. But underneath all the fun times and laughter was a marriage struggling to re-establish itself after childbirth. Frustration mounted as we both felt like we weren't being supported. We were exhausting our energy, yet barely keeping our heads above water. It's hard to lend a helping hand when you both feel like you're drowning in duties.

Communication was never a problem. We would talk often about expectations and our roles and responsibilities. Yet we couldn't seem to see eye-to-eye. Leanne wanted more help at home. I wanted more freedom to pursue business endeavors. It's not as if I felt it was beneath me to do domestic work. As a full-time professional, full-time father and part-time writer, many household chores had to compete with other pressing obligations. I prioritized them in descending order. When it came down to making a business deal or making my bed, I chose the revenue generating task. In my estimation, I could spend the rest of my life constantly making my bed and never be one step closer to our goal of financial freedom.

Prior to Zoe arriving, we established Cover Three Publishing, a small independent publishing house. Our desire was to become entrepreneurs. We limped along for the first few years until we became more established. Once we gained our footing, we began to turn a profit. Still our publishing business wasn't earning enough to sustain us, so by day I worked my corporate job and at night I worked on my exit strategy—writing. That meant writing until 4

AM, going to sleep for a few hours, waking up and doing the same thing all over again. It was tough, but seeing light at the end of the tunnel gave me solace.

Leanne's job was to hold down the fort. Take care of our daughter and other responsibilities to keep home life running smoothly. I was far from an overbearing husband who expected dinner on the table when he got home or even that dinner needed to be cooked. All I asked was that she communicated. That way I could pick up food on the way home if needed. I wasn't the type of husband who walked in the door wearing a white glove expecting the house to be so clean that I could eat off the floor. I was pretty laid back and self-sufficient. I didn't require much support. I washed and folded my own clothes. If needed, I ironed them for work. I would wake up and make myself breakfast in the morning. At night, we had an agreement whoever cooked the other cleaned the dishes. I was extremely diplomatic in my approach to marriage, so when Leanne complained about lack of support it seemed unfair to me.

Two years after Zoe, our son, Caleb, was born and most of our issues were magnified times two. If we previously were up to our necks with responsibilities, we were now fully submerged and drowning. A second child meant even less time to focus on our relationship and our arguments became more frequent and boisterous. Cussing and yelling was never a part of our lover's bouts. We fought like verbal boxers, a lot of quick jabs and an occasional sucker punch. A few shots would cut deep, but we rarely went to sleep angry at each other. Even if we didn't resolve the argument, we'd call a truce and revisit the conversation the next day—a pact we made in the early stages of marriage, along with never involving outsiders in our relationship disputes.

Even though having children put a strain on our marriage, it also galvanized us, creating a paradoxical relationship between our marriage pre and post kids. Our children produced a synergy within our marriage where the sum was clearly greater than its individual parts. There was no way we could look at each other and not see wife and mother, husband and father. Neither of us was willing to surrender our titles for baby daddy or baby mama.

We were fighting not to lose our identity within the marriage. It's one of the deadliest threats to a union. There were dreams we both had prior to meeting each other. Some undoubtedly would be placed on the back burner. However, some life goals were non-negotiable. Becoming a professional writer held a sacred place in my heart that I refused to surrender. Leanne met me at a time of transition as I struggled to define myself after my football career ended. Writing was my therapy. It helped me deal with the feeling of a rug being pulled out from under my feet and provided me with a new passion.

Ultimately, to let marriage or fatherhood douse my dreams would be detrimental to the family. If I allowed married life to deter my dreams over time I would harbor resentment. Every time I looked at my wife and kids they would be a constant reminder of my shortcomings. I refused to allow those thoughts to manifest in my heart. I continued to pushback against Leanne when she asked me to put down the pen and postpone my current projects, in spite of the challenges it caused in the present, to preserve our future.

Leanne, on the other hand, was completely consumed by the kids. Catering to me—or even to herself—became an afterthought. She read book after book about motherhood. She purchased an immersion blender to make organic baby food. She was anal about the kids staying on their meal, napping and bedtime schedule; even though she was getting little sleep and wasn't eating regularly. She lost a significant amount of weight. She was stressed and over-whelmed by her new role. Being a stay-at-home mom was taking its toll, to the point that she would be waiting at the door, ready to hand off baby Caleb when I returned home. I would've felt sympa-thy for her, but the stresses of the corporate world didn't allow me to recognize that she was dying inside. All I felt was added stress and pressure in a place that was supposed to be my safe haven. I started sitting in the car for a half hour to decompress before walk-ing in the house and jumping right into daddy mode.

My feelings were always that while I could certainly be doing more, I was at least augmenting her duties by helping around the house and with the kids. But who was helping me? How many emails had she written? How many meetings had she run? How many workshops had she conducted? How many speaking engage-ments had she arranged? How many hours had she spent locked away working on manuscripts? The answer to all of the above was "none." My honest thought was "what does she have to complain about?"

It wasn't until one night while I was on a business trip, I called home and Leanne answered the phone drowning in tears, that I finally heard her plea. I could barely make out what she was saying, but it was clear that my wife was hurting. I felt helpless on the other end of the phone, listening to her sob, unable to comfort her. When I came back to town, we sat down and discussed our future. Leanne expressed she was tired of feeling like a single mother. She asked me to consider a career move to a position with less travel. I agreed. I realized that I had lost focus. So much of my energy was being expended chasing after my career that I had completely stopped pursuing my wife. I was guilty as charged. Leanne had sacrificed her career, health and sanity and I was too busy wrapped up in my work to notice.

Prior to having kids, much of her identity was found in her work. Leanne's dad groomed her to be business minded. She was preparing for her MBA when we learned she was pregnant with Zoe. As a result, school was put on hold. I left the door open for her to decide if she wanted to go back to school or work. Feeling like the stay-at-home mom role was too taxing, I suggested Leanne consider rejoining the workforce. I thought getting dolled up for work and interacting with adults might be enough to help her regain her identity.

We hired a nanny and she went back to work. She worked for seven months, but the position was experimental. Sales results didn't meet expectations so the position was terminated. We were back to square one! However, the short work experience exposed just how much we both valued having someone at home. Even with a nanny it became increasingly difficult to plan our schedules. She had work commitments on nights and weekends. I was flying from city to city for various business functions. Our nanny was sometimes working twelve-hour days and the kids were only seeing us in passing. It was not the lifestyle we envisioned for our family, so the decision was made for Leanne to come back home, with the caveat that we would keep our nanny for a short time longer.

To date I'm unsure how our third child, Tori Christine, came to be. Almost immediately after Caleb was born, sex was all but absent. This third child may very well be the first ever conceived through osmosis. I'm being facetious, but sex was infrequent. Not only was sex at an all-time low, physical touch was minimal. Time alone came at a premium. To go on a date meant we had to factor in the cost of our activities along with the babysitter. We tried to remain frugal, so date nights often consisted of takeout and a Netflix movie after the kids went to bed. Exhausted from our daily routines, one or both of us typically wouldn't make it through the movie. If sex was on the menu, I had to settle for a nocturnal emission.

Sex has never been a large part of our relationship, even from the beginning. Within days of meeting Leanne, she almost derailed our destiny with the revelation that she was abstinent. Leanne had been saving herself for marriage, but fell short on a few occasions in her previous relationship. It haunted her deeply. Therefore, she wanted to make it clear that I would have no part of her cookie before marriage. I was devastated and honestly had no plans of pursuing a relationship with her.

At the time, I was entertaining other women so I figured I would keep her around just as a friend. However, we began spending a significant amount of time together. We would go out to eat and talk for hours over a meal. We would workout together, competing and challenging each other to get better. Most notably, she invited me to church and we worshiped side-by-side. Through her I found Christ. This quality time together took our relationship to a deeper level than sex ever could.

Beyond her celibacy there was something unique about her that kept me intrigued. She was different, in ways that were obvious. My shallow attempts at impressing her failed miserably. Materialistic things other women deemed so important, she placed no value in. There was nothing fake about her. More importantly, there was nothing fake about me in her presence. I had grown accustomed to being on stage around women. But I was tired of the guy I was expected to be as an athlete—the egotistical multi-woman juggler. She allowed me to let my guard down and exit stage left.

I bared my naked self to her and she embraced me wholeheartedly, every artsy-fartsy, Pro-Black part of me. I found comfort in her arms. She was as deep as the ocean's floor. Her depth gave me the confidence to set sail with her, trusting that no storm would capsize us.

After two months I had severed all communication with other women and we were moving fast toward a serious relationship. After a year of dating we were engaged, but there would be another year and a half before our wedding day. In total, I was abstinent for two years, eight months, seven days, three hours and thirty-three seconds, not that I was counting. The first eight months I tried every creative way to get her to sleep with me, to no avail. I lit candles and broke out strawberries. I dimmed the lights and played Marvin Gaye. I was terrible, but she was faithful in her beliefs and ways.

As I grew deeper in my spirituality, I stopped trying to set snares to trap her. I recognized the beauty in our wait and began rowing in the same direction. The struggle was real; still we learned much about each other during the process. That period served as the foundation of our union. It was built on a true friendship. This foundation would prove to be crucial as we battled through critical seasons in our marriage.

Once we crossed the threshold of marriage, I expected our sex life to explode, instead, and much to my chagrin, it fizzled out in Jamaica on our honeymoon. Raised in a Christian family, Leanne had been conditioned to view sex as taboo. She spent her entire adolescent and young adult life fighting to preserve her virginity and avoiding sex. All of a sudden she was married and expected to turn on her sexuality and perform with the flip of a switch. She was extremely reserved and noticeably apprehensive. There were still remnants of shame surrounding sex.

We struggled in the bedroom as Leanne continued to work through her reconditioning. Sex was a little awkward at times and clumsy. Even though our marriage certificate gave Leanne the freedom to indulge, a part of her subconsciously felt engaging in sex was sleazy. It took over a year of prayer and give-and-take, massaging each other's expectations to make us sexually attuned to each other.

Beyond sex, we both entered marriage with some clear, albeit unwritten expectations. We did our due diligence to uncover any unrealistic beliefs in premarital counseling, still they remained concealed. Only with time and children did our unmet expectations surface. When they did, we realized we both thought we were marrying a different person. I realized that I expected Leanne to be Suzy Homemaker. I wanted her to handle her role of stay-at-home mother with more ease. Never did I envision her struggling so mightily. I expected flawless execution of her motherly duties.

The primary reason why I love her, but also struggle to understand her is because she doesn't fit any mold. She's not the happy homemaker that will be content managing the home front. Nor is she the Type A career woman, driven by status and power, who's determined to be the CEO of a Fortune 500. She's an equal blend of both. The duality of her personality made finding a solution to our problems complicated.

Though she will disagree, I always felt Leanne expected me to be less ambitious and more content with just earning a living. She didn't expect to marry a perpetual moon chaser. She wanted some-one who was more supportive and less fixated on personal goals. In our arguments, I would often say to her "I think you would love me more if I was a steel mill worker," the type of guy who puts on his hard hat every morning and grinds through a twelve to four-teen-hour shift; day after day. This guy is predictable. This guy is simple. He is content with the life he has been given. The only problem is that I grew up dirt-poor without a pot to piss in. I had no desire of leaving the same legacy for my children.

As we continued to have reoccurring arguments, it became clear that we had different visions for our future. We both wanted to live comfortably, but disagreed as to the extent, as well as how to attain it. Raised in the projects on the south side of Chicago in Robbins (IL), I only knew one way to approach my goals. The streets taught me to be relentless in my pursuit. Never take "no" for an answer or allow any hurdles to impede my progress. Leanne was raised in a completely different environment in White suburbia, one more conducive to positivity. The same challenges I faced that forced me to view life through a distorted lens were absent from her picture. This childhood provided her the luxury of coming up for air from time to time. I was conditioned to keep my head down and grind it out until success brought me to the surface.

Ironically, Leanne's dad came from Jamaica with only the clothes on his back. He worked hard, putting himself through school and putting in long hours at the office to ensure his family lived well, creating a new legacy in his lineage that will live on forever. I always found it paradoxical that Leanne would clamor for me to pursue fewer projects when everything she was afforded came from her dad's unwaivering drive and ambition. I wanted nothing more than to provide for my children what was provided to her.

Ultimately, how we've been able to see past our differences and still find happiness is through prayer and our relationship with God. Prayer helps us keep life in proper perspective. Even though some challenging aspects of our relationship haven't changed, a shift in perspective has helped us view them differently, resulting in a better attitude toward each other. Also, the more we communicated and verbalized our concerns the more we began to notice a common theme. Almost all of our marital problems were self-inflicted.

The majority of our arguments stemmed from our children or our careers. We had within our ability to choose whether or not to have children or pursue a certain career. We made the conscious effort to have multiple kids. Leanne dared to venture down the path of home schooling. I chose to stay in the corporate world while simultaneously working to build a company. We weren't victims of circumstance. It wasn't as if life had dealt us a bad hand. Almost everything we were struggling with was positive.

Once this epiphany was finally able to sink in, we stopped taking for granted all the blessings in our life, including each other. We sought help from the outside. However, it didn't come in the form of a marriage counselor. It came in the form of Leanne's mother. She was recently divorced from Leanne's dad and living alone. We invited her to come live with us to lighten Leanne's load. It also gave me more flexibility to pursue business ventures and provided the kids with priceless interaction with their grandmother.

Aside from seeking help, we worked to rekindle our romance.

We made time for each other. We sat down and had lengthy conversations about our future and strived to come to an agreement. We discussed where we planned to be in ten years. How much money did we want in our savings? In what city should we raise our children? Did we want more children? Are we keeping our single-income family structure? What are we willing to sacrifice? What is non-negotiable? Once we aligned our visions and set our oars back rowing in the same direction, our interaction improved. It reduced the amount of repetitive arguments that were sucking the energy out of our relationship. We are still a work in progress. However, we view our marriage as more than a legal document that can be shredded. It is a sacred covenant we both deemed worth preserving.

Fake Housewives of Black America

A few years ago, Leanne and I were on our way to my ten-year college reunion. Although a reminder that I was getting old[er], I was actually looking forward to reliving college life for the evening: frat parties at Norris, the late night stealth bike rides to the sorority quads, and the post-game parties at the football house. Beyond reminiscing about the past, the reunion provided a chance to learn about the various career paths we'd all taken since graduating. With the growth of social media, some of the suspense was spoiled, but the game was nonetheless on to determine who would be unofficially crowned most successful.

Success was also measured by if you were married, and how well you married, placing spouses on display to be measured against their equivalents. We arrived fashionably late, as usual, and began mingling. As we worked our way through the crowd talking and laughing something became readily apparent. Every time we engaged in conversation and the subject shifted to occupations, Leanne would shrink. She would begrudgingly murmur, "I'm a stay-at-home mom." hoping no one would question further. No one did. Because in today's society there is little interest in it. There is nothing exciting or intriguing about changing diapers and keeping house. Investing fully in your children to help ensure they have the proper spiritual and educational foundation is not as glamorous or sexy as attorney or investment banker.

Stay-at-home mom is now a shameful term; however, the word "housewife" has become idolized, hijacked by a series of reality shows starring women who are indeed allergic to Ajax. By definition, a housewife is a married woman whose main occupation is caring for her family, managing household affairs, and doing housework. Ironically, none of the women in these shows embody the characteristics of a traditional housewife. Their days are spent driving around in their Mercedes going to spas and lunch dates with their fellow housewives or pursuing various business endeavors.

Rarely do these shows capture women performing domestic activities or spending significant time with their children. Much of those duties have been delegated to the nanny, housekeeper, personal chef or occasionally the birthday event planner. Kids and spouses are glorified extras in the show, playing minor roles in the overall series. They are simply an accessory to be worn on the housewives' arm like their latest designer handbag. Some of these "housewives" are no longer even married, instead choosing to play the field and building an empire.

After giving birth, some career women are opting to leave the corporate world to invest time in raising their children, at least through the developmental stage prior to kindergarten—as my wife did. Though we are not "rich," I earn a comfortable living. But I can assure you her day is not spent working out with her personal trainer or getting a massage.

Truthfully, there are times she doesn't even leave the house. With three children, aged five and under, there is enough to do just to get through the day. Stay-at-home motherhood is not for the weak. It takes a special kind of woman. This is why when I'm asked what my wife does, I am clear to state that while she doesn't bring home a paycheck, it doesn't mean she doesn't work hard or contribute.

The false belief that the content in these shows represent an accurate depiction of the cast members' lives is alarming. They take cues from a producer on set no different than a big-screen actor. Yet, this "fly on the wall" strategy, a media ploy designed to present reality series as an authentic and unscripted intimate glimpse into other people's lives, has been successfully executed for years. Show producers create just enough believable situations to hook the audience, then they use the storylines to bombard viewers with one exaggerated drama after another.

Believability is vital to the female public adopting showbiz fantasy as reality and ushering artificial concepts of marriage and motherhood into mainstream society. Not satisfied with living vicariously through these housewives, some women are in search of a husband who can help provide "the good life." The show functions to reduce the wealthy lifestyle to the acceptable standard of living, creating unrealistic expectations for most single and married women. After watching these women spending their days shopping, nights socializing and summers on private islands, even traditional career women find themselves envious, longing for the day they can trade in their fifty-hour workweek for jet skis and rum punch.

The result is a growing group of single women digging for gold, selling themselves short, in pursuit of a cash cow to help kick-start their business venture—via marriage or a lucrative divorce settlement. Specific to the Black community, he has to come in the form of an entertainer or superstar athlete because those are the professionals viewed at the pinnacle of Black high society. Younger generations of Black girls are also being influenced by these images—either through direct viewing or copycat family members—creating a new Black female consciousness. Congruent with the wave of New-Age feminism, these women are viewed as torch bearers—willfully defiant in their resistance of social barriers relating to their gender and race—and trendsetters.

People are getting smarter and so are computers. My five-year-old daughter can navigate through my smartphone as well, if not better, than I can. We continue to evolve as a society and introduce new technology and new philosophies causing a cultural shift. But all that is new does not represent progress. There is nothing progressive or trailblazing about a group of thirty and forty plus women, drunk, fighting, and behaving like high school seniors. It is unethical to manufacture conflict for increased ratings on a reality show, not to mention, unrealistic.

These women look in the mirror and see the reflection of a strong independent woman. However, their persona more accurately reflects Rosie the Ratchet than Rosie the Riveter. Producers paint these women as aggressive movers and shakers willing to risk everything, including friendships, to close a business deal. It's unclear how this unbecoming behavior represents progress.

Greed has been woven into our society since the beginning of time. The "men do it why can't women?" argument is shallow. It's neither good for the goose nor the gander. Subscribing to the belief that since men behave corruptly or unjust is justification for women to follow suit, means you categorically believe two wrongs make a right. In the context of racism, I guess that means Black people should begin burning crosses on White folks' lawns in an effort to return the favor. That's just how destructive and counterproductive the notion that women's liberation is found in societal degradation seems.

TV media is a powerful tool. There are people who have never left the boundaries of their city or state, and the television becomes their cultural curator providing a single window into mainstream society through the lens of reality TV, drama series and sitcoms. We don't need any more shows that perpetuate a stereotype that Black women are angry, emasculating, hyper-sexual beings. We need models of stable family units not broken homes, no matter how palatial they may be.

THE IMPACT

IMPACT [im-pakt]: the strong effect or influence that something has on a situation or person.

It's impossible to overstate the impact the rise of the Independent Black Woman and subsequent single mother has had on the Black community. "If a kingdom is divided against itself, that kingdom cannot stand. If a house is dived against itself, that house cannot stand." (Mark 3:24-25). This Biblical certainty underscores the prodigious plight of urban Black America: fiscal retardation, crime proliferation, chronic gun violence, perpetual teenage pregnancy, high illiteracy and high school dropout rates. There is no panacea for the malignant ailments plaguing the Black community. However, if such a cure-all existed, the remedy wouldn't be found in the molecular structure of a man-made drug. It would be harnessed in the intrinsic value of a traditional man-led family structure.

Perhaps I missed how exactly division represents progress for the Black community. In a society where our mere existence seems problematic to the mainstream, fighting within can only result in implosion. To be independent is to be free, not subject to another's authority or dependent upon someone or something for aid or support. But in a healthy relationship both man and woman are mutually dependent upon each other for physical, emotional and spiritual support. Black women have become so enamored with the persona of the Independent Black Woman that the concept of interdependence has become bastardized—relegated to women who aren't strong enough to sustain themselves.

95

The criticism is that a woman who depends on her man is weak and a man who depends on his woman is soft. But by our innate makeup we are designed to be in companionship. God never intended for us to walk alone. For that very reason, after creating Adam, God made Eve. Developing financial independence doesn't absolve Black women from the perils of this life that are sure to come. When the rain comes, we usually look for shelter in the arms of loved ones—primarily a significant other. To truly be independent as a Black woman (or man) means to reject what is a part of our spiritual DNA.

The strong correlation between the growth of the Independent Black Woman and the rise of the single Black mother suggests Black fathers have diminishing value. Many Independent Black Women are products of successive fatherless generations, giving the impression that fathers are optional. However, a father's presence is absolutely necessary for balance. Some liberals are attempting to push an agenda suggesting that two parents of any gender is all a child needs. Not true. A child, male or female, requires nurturing from both his mother and father to be balanced. Regardless, the value of a father cannot be measured simply by what he brings to the table; it also must be measured through what is often avoided by his presence.

As opportunistic young men back in the days, my boys and I sought after girls with "daddy issues." They were viewed as easy low-hanging fruit. It was done with such regularity that daddy questions became a part of the unofficial prescreening.

"How you doin' baby girl? Blah…blah…blah. You live with both parents?"

"Yeah. My mama and daddy been married almost twenty years."

"Oh that's great! Okay. Well it was nice meetin' you."
Next girl…

"How you doin' love? Blah…blah…blah. Yo daddy be mean to your boyfriends?"

"I've never met my father."

"Damn, I'm sorry to hear that. You wanna go somewhere and chill?"

If a teenage girl whose father is absent goes looking for love in all the wrong places and ends up pregnant, the root of the problem is not promiscuity, it's abandonment. Children with abandonment issues that go unaddressed, become adults with abandonment issues. A girl who has a healthy relationship with her father will typically grow to become a woman with a healthy relationship with sex and the opposite sex.

The rate of unwed births has remained consistent and so has the rate of unplanned births. In 2011, 45 percent of the 6.1 million pregnancies in the U.S. were unintended (i.e., the pregnancy was unwanted or mistimed at the time of birth). Black women had the highest unintended pregnancy rate of any racial or ethnic group, more than double that of non-Hispanic white women. This trend suggests some single Black women have a casual relationship with contraceptives. I understand that sometimes circumstances change and some women's plans are altered because their boyfriend decides to abandon ship in the eleventh hour, forcing young women into the position of single mother. However, those women on the other end of the spectrum who make a unilateral decision to bring a Black child into the world and intentionally raise that child as a single parent are committing a selfish act. With all the disparaging information at our fingertips outlining the challenges Black children raised in single-mother homes experience, the decision to deliberately create life under those circumstances could only be for self-interest.

Some affluent single Black women view children as a consumer product. As long as they can afford a child why shouldn't they have one? They believe waiting on a husband might kill their chances of motherhood. It relinquishes a woman's control and places her at the mercy of a man. This goes against the philosophies of the New-Age Black feminists, which is centered around being the master of your own destiny. If a woman wants a child, she is encouraged to have her baby—regardless of her marital status. Besides, in today's society there is nothing immoral or pathological about having a child out of wedlock. However, the negative trends associated with fatherless homes are not limited to urban Black America. They are widespread, crossing racial and economic barriers (especially when controlling for neighborhood statistics). Why? Because neither a butler nor maid can replace the presence of a father.

Ninety percent of all homeless and runaway children are from fatherless homes. Seventy-five percent of all adolescent patients in chemical abuse centers come from fatherless homes. Sixty-three percent of youth suicides are from fatherless homes. All three of which: runaways, drug abuse and suicides are recognized as affluent family problems. All three of which are tied to the same common denominator…unhappiness. The same reason a young girl would abuse drugs or take her life is the same reason why she would flee home in the middle of the night. Beyond profound unhappiness, there is a void in her life that is typically present due to a father's absence.

To fully appreciate the negative impact single-mother households have on the Black community, one has to measure its effect on the most vulnerable members of the most disadvantaged community—poor Black children.

Children are like sponges. They absorb everything around them. They cannot reason like an adult to understand what a positive or negative influence is and filter accordingly. They rely solely on their parents (or guardians) to teach them how to distinguish between the two. However, some parents have been so desensitized to their environment that the line between the two becomes blurred. Even when parents are supposedly limiting their child's exposure, too much is still being exposed.

Parents take for granted the heightened senses of a child. They constantly underestimate their child's ability to learn. By doing so, the problem becomes twofold; parents present less formal learning tools to their children and unintentionally bombard them with more useless information than they can handle.

Even when a child is too young to be sat down and talked to about relationships, they are old enough to observe what they see and form their own thoughts. As a mother, if every few weeks or so, you bring home a new boyfriend, what kind of message is that sending to your five-year-old daughter? She might not be able to fully comprehend the situation, but understand she is internalizing these images and taking note of your behavior. As your daughter grows older and starts dating men, she might not remember what she saw, but she will use her moral compass to help guide her. Somewhere tucked away in her subconscious, she will have "multiple male companions" as an acceptable practice. Ten to 15 years later, it would not be unreasonable to suggest she has a greater risk of being in a similar single-mother predicament.

Studies show babies and young children learn at a rate that will never be matched, at any other stage in their lives. These formative years provide the fundamental education that helps shape the child's perspective and understanding. Most of what you believe right now, as an adult, is a direct reflection of what you learned as a child.

The two major arenas, in which a child is fundamentally educated, are in school and at home. Both are places where a child spends the majority of his or her early life. Home provides the primary education and school the secondary. Together, they help provide a child with basic academic knowledge and life skills that serve as the child's foundation. That foundation is then used, as the base for which all other knowledge is built upon.

Unfortunately, there are many Black children growing up in poverty who live in single-parent homes; where their fathers are nowhere to be found and their mothers are performing Herculean tasks just to stay afloat. Ultimately, the child raises himself (or herself) and the streets, and all the filth in it, become their primary education, filling the void left by the absence of parents. That is the family system far too many of our young Black children find themselves forced into.

As vast as these issues may seem, they are all interlinked with absent fathers acting as ground zero—the epicenter of all problems. The aftermath of the fatherless Black home implosion has left devastation in five major areas: education, crime, imprisonment, teenage pregnancy and wealth, all of which are surefire ways to perpetuate generational poverty.

Lack of quality education results in lack of employment opportunities. Lack of gainful employment results in subsequent criminal activity. Criminal behavior results in imprisonment. Imprisonment further limits your opportunity for employment, wealth and mobility, sentencing you to life in poverty. Teenage pregnancy ties back into lack of education and produces similar hapless endings.

I concede that not all two-parent homes are healthy and capable of bearing ripe fruit. Sometimes the best alternative is for the parents to separate, especially when the relationship turns violent or abusive. Abusive fathers would be hard pressed to provide a positive influence. Regardless, the empirical data remains disheartening for Black children raised in fatherless households.

Education Gap

Each year, between 750,000 to one million students drop out of high school in the United States. Seventy-one percent of all high school dropouts live in fatherless homes. These statistics alone should give pause to anyone considering raising a child solo.

Additionally, 85 percent of all children who exhibit behavioral disorders come from fatherless homes. Behavior disorders become problematic in two ways. They either lead to out-of-school suspensions and expulsions (which are three-times higher for Black students compared to Whites) or place students on the special education (SPED) track over-labeling many as handicap—a designation that follows them throughout their scholastic career.

A conflict of interest created by unintended consequences of government support for the disabled further worsens the problem. Poor single mothers find themselves in a position to significantly increase their monthly income through the federal Supplemental Security Income (SSI) program by allowing their daughter or son to be branded disabled. Under the program cash payments can be made to the guardian of the recipient and depending on the state, the family becomes eligible for added payments through the state, Medicaid, food stamps and other social programs—indeed a struggling mother's winning lottery ticket.

I view education as the key to unlimited possibilities. Without it, career options become woefully limited, and the future can be grim. With education, however, the opportunities become endless. High school dropouts commit about 70 percent of all crimes in America. In this global economy, America struggles to compete with cheap foreign labor. The U.S. is slowly moving away from industrial manufacturing. Relatively good paying labor jobs that only require a high school diploma are becoming obsolete. They are being replaced by more service oriented cerebral jobs that require a Bachelor's degree or higher. As such, quality of education becomes equally as important. Access to a top-notch high school education can determine college acceptance or readiness.

There is more to career success than just having a college degree, just as there is more to swimming than just holding your breath. Swimming requires technique and form, but if you fail to first learn how to hold your breath you will never be able to swim. It is one of the basic fundamentals. I view college in the same way in respect to starting a career. There are other professional skills you must acquire to be successful, but without a college degree it will be almost impossible to even begin the journey.

With more and more people attaining Master's and Doctorate degrees, an undergraduate degree has now become equivalent to a high school diploma. Not in the sense that someone with a Bachelor's degree and someone with a high school diploma are equally qualified, but in the sense that the value of a Bachelor's degree has depreciated considerably.

It's like the value of money relative to inflation, as inflation surges the value of a dollar decreases. Over time the same dollar that used to buy you a bottled drink out of the vending machine now will barely purchase you a small bag of chips. Each year costs increase with the price of raw materials, labor and freight. Subsequently, the consumer sees an incremental increase in the cost of his favorite soda or potato chips.

Likewise, each year thousands of students graduate from college, making the pool of qualified applicants more abundant. This weakens the value of a Bachelor's degree in the corporate world. The same position you could have held ten years ago with a Bachelor's degree now requires an MBA.

High Crime

There is nothing earth-shattering about the notion that poverty breeds many offspring—prostitution, burglary, armed robbery, drug trafficking—resulting in high crime. Crime is viewed as a necessary evil. It becomes a survival mechanism used for self-preservation for those born into an unfavorable status. Their status typically reflects: poor, Black and fatherless.

At the intersection of poverty and crime is fatherlessness, exacerbating the presence of both in America. Children living in fatherless homes are almost four-times more likely to be poor. Twelve percent of children in married families are living in poverty, compared to 44 percent of children in single-mother households. With 67 percent of Black children being raised in homes absent of a father, it's obvious how Black poverty gets cycled down through generations.

Black people are disproportionately poor, fundamentally, to no fault of their own. Regardless, this places Black children, especially those from fatherless homes, at higher risk to commit crimes—twice as likely to be exact. In an environment unconducive to positive growth and where a mother is required to work constantly to make ends meet, often there is no one home to care for the youth. Children are free to roam. Subsequently, crime becomes a result of opportunity and boredom. We've all been guilty of "dumbdom," dumb decisions made out of boredom. However, the stakes are higher for Black youth—especially Black male youth. One joyride in a stolen car to break the monotony of the summer could leave you locked up all winter.

104

Children are habitual line crossers. No matter how much leeway you afford them they will find a way to infringe upon the No Trespassing zone. It's in a child's nature—though some more than others. My son requires redirection more often than my daughters. As a Black man, I take it as my personal responsibility to remind him of his boundaries so society doesn't have to in ways that are unforgiving. I can't fathom the struggles Caleb would face having to figure out life without me. My presence changes the entire atmosphere around the house. He understands there is someone he loves and respects that is superior to him in the castle. This relationship dynamic alone could change the fate of countless young Black men. Many who are living in single-mother homes struggle with authority. They assume the role of the "man of the house" prematurely and never learn to respect the natural hierarchy. This lack of respect for authority has far reaching ramifications in society.

Beyond my son, my wife and daughters rest easier when daddy is home. They understand part of my job is to protect them and that I will embrace this duty with my last breath. Unfortunately, there are many daughters living in homes without a father, which increases the potential for sexual violence. Young girls living without one of their natural parents are at greater risk of sexual abuse. Typically, children are sexually abused by adults who are family members, friends of the family, or someone with reoccurring interaction, for instance, a teacher, pastor, or a coach. Having no biological father around opens the door to sexual predators, often in the form of step-fathers. Most studies conclude that girls living with a male adult in the house who is not their natural father are at high risk of sexual abuse, stepfathers just happen to be the most common occurrence. Predators sense vulnerability. The lack of a male scent is a dead giveaway.

Fatherless homes create crime problems that are twofold: not only do they increase the amount of crimes committed by children; they increase the amount of sex crimes committed against children.

Mass Incarceration

Seventy percent of juveniles in state-operated institutions come from fatherless homes. However, incarceration in the Black community is one clear area in which the impact of fatherlessness gets overshadowed by the effect of outside forces targeting Black men and leading to mass imprisonment. The rise of the For-Profit prison industry has resulted in a prison-industrial complex by which the American economy profits from the jailing of its citizens. A disturbing proposition and clear conflict of interest, nonetheless, this practice has been successfully adopted with Black men as the chief focus.

In the age of mass incarceration, little effort is required from a Black man to find himself locked behind bars. In fact, an inexplicable one in every three Black males born today can expect to serve a stint in prison in their lifetime—based on current incarceration rates. Too often, jail time for minor infractions is becoming an unofficial life sentence, subjecting ex-cons to limitations of their civil rights and prolonged oversight by the criminal justice system. This in turn limits the rehabilitated members of our society from obtaining gainful employment, which pushes them back into the felonious underworld. Then the cycle repeats...prison-parole-prison.

People often attempt to assign a color to crime, but race, isolated, has little influence on criminal activity—though it plays a key role in the punishment for the crime. Criminality, in general, is a socioeconomic problem caused by lack of basic necessities and opportunity. A high percentage of poverty and fatherless homes in the Black community, coupled with often minor criminal activity, gives the false impression of an innate criminal chromosome of a downtrodden subgroup, perpetuating a stereotype and fueling a bias in the judicial system. In 1971, when President Nixon declared a "War on Drugs" it was, in part, designed to target Black people. That's why America finds itself with an egregiously disproportionate 37 percent of its male inmate population comprised of Black men.

For instance, the disparity in time served for crack cocaine possession (more commonly distributed in the Black community) versus the powder form of the same substance (a more affluent party drug in the White community) is significantly greater. Those convicted of crack possession received 50 percent more jail time. That's assuming the White drug possessor is caught. Given the one-sidedness in the way black communities are policed compared to surrounding white neighborhoods, that's a gratuitous assumption.

Beyond convicts, these men are humans, many of whom have children who are now forced to grow up fatherless. I'm far from the delusion that all inmates would make positive role models. However, if ten percent are quality fathers, their presence is needed at home for all the reasons stated above and below.

Teenage Pregnancy

One afternoon several years back while I was on the 'L' train in Chicago, I overheard a conversation between two young Black girls. One of them was with her two kids and the other was by herself. I wasn't paying attention to their conversation until I heard the young girl with kids say to the other, "Girl you 25 and you ain't got no kids yet...what you waiting on?" Her friend gave some plausible excuse and they continued their conversation. It's this type of backward thinking that keeps young Black girls impoverished. Here was a young single mother on the train with her two kids, ridiculing her friend for not perpetuating a problem in the Black community. What would be more tragic is if that young lady took the peer pressure to heart and set out on a search for her baby daddy.

Teen pregnancy has dropped significantly over the past decade, yet racial disparities persist. Young Black women who become teenage mothers are like POWs locked away in a makeshift prison who then decide to cuff themselves to an immoveable object, making an escape increasingly less probable and turning a dire situation even bleaker. With the amount of contraceptives available today, there are few excuses for a young woman to "accidentally" become pregnant. She is either being careless or flirting with the idea of being a teenage mother. In both cases, she is sentencing herself to a life full of struggles and in all likelihood...poverty. More than half of all mothers on welfare had their first child as a teenager. Why? Parenthood is the leading reason teen girls drop out of school. Fifty percent of teen mothers never graduate from high school. Less than two percent of teen moms earn a college degree by age thirty. Roughly, 25 percent of teen moms have a second child within two years of their first baby, compounding the precipitous downward spiral.

The common denominator in 71 percent of teenage pregnancies is single-parent homes. It's understood that most single-parent homes are mother-led so essentially we arrive back at fatherlessness. To add insult to injury, eight out of ten teen dads don't marry the mother of their child, perpetuating a generational curse of fatherlessness in the family's heritage.

The child is merely the result of an action. The root of the problem lies in the unmet needs of a daughter from her father. The lack of affection from a father can lead to what's commonly referred to as "daddy issues." Pick your cliché: looking for love in all the wrong places or seeking validation in a relationship. Many young ladies who grew up without a father have lingering abandonment issues, causing them to seek love from every charming man who pursues them—especially young teenage girls in the early stages of their dating lives. Often, they will date much older men who are more like father figures, subconsciously looking to them to provide the emotional support and protection lacked by a physically or emotionally absent father. This pattern often leads to disappointment. Older men are usually more sexually advanced and often controlling, resulting in sexual exploitation and physical or verbal abuse. After being let down by enough men, some ladies will become jaded and give up on dating.

The Wealth Gap

The greatest deed a Black woman can do for the Black community is marry a Black man. Countless studies have proven that married men are more successful. Married men's hearts are healthier. Those with children are also viewed as more stable by employers. In general, married men work more hours per week than their single peers, resulting in more income for hourly workers and more career capital for salaried employees. Married men are more career-focused and responsible. They are less likely to quit a current job before lining up a new one. Marriage acts as a natural income stimulant encouraging men to maximize their earning potential. Most of all they benefit from much needed sound advice from their spouses.

Successful Black husbands result in successful Black families. Successful Black families result in a healthy Black community. Despite Black women entering the workforce and earning respectable incomes, the wealth gap between Black and White families has grown exponentially over the years. Wealth is measured by household income and assets minus debts. With unwed Black women at double the rate of White women, the lack of a husband's assets in the Black community is the root cause of the growing gap. From 1984 to 2007, the wealth gap between Whites and Blacks increased fourfold from $20,000 to $95,000. Post-Recession, from 2010 to 2013, the median wealth of non-Hispanic White households increased from $138,600 to $141,900, or 2.4 percent. Meanwhile, the median wealth of non-Hispanic Black households fell 33.7 percent from \$16,600 in 2010 to \$11,000 in 2013. Certainly, some of the problems are driven by public policy, but the catalyst is lack of marriage, with lack of education coming in at a close second.

Education and wealth have a direct correlation. It is not by coincidence that most rich people are well-educated, or that most people living in poverty are not. My maternal grandmother, the matriarch of our family, had only a sixth-grade education. Born in the 1920s into a sharecropping family in the south, a mere two generations removed from slavery, Granny was forced to drop out of school to help tend the field. Picking cotton would consume the rest of her childhood. In 1942, during the second wave of the Great Migration, the family moved north to hyper-segregated Chicago that boxed Blacks into ghettos. They would settle in a small village called Robbins on the southwest outskirts.

Just shy of 17, with only a sixth-grade education, female and Black, Granny was limited in the types of jobs she was eligible to work. With many men overseas fighting in World War II, she was able to find a manufacturing job working at Universal Hat & Cap MFG; a hat factory supplying headgear for Cub Scouts, Webelos, Scouts and Explorers. She would remain there for over 30 years until the company went out of business.

In the early sixties, Cook County built a low-income public housing project in Robbins. Granny was now a single-mother raising four children and struggling to make ends meet, so she moved into the project shortly after it was built. She would live there for more than 40 years. Two generations of descendants would live in public housing—including my mother and her children. We were by no means unique as many of our neighbors had similar tenures.

Coming from the South, where Granny lived on a plantation

in a one-room shack, the projects represented advancement. They were modern, all the utilities functioned properly and the rent was affordable. The combined comfort of government subsidy and lack of career opportunity created a recipe for perpetual poverty. This paradigm remains consistent across most Black families in America who are victims of a pervasive government-sponsored dependency, permanently affixed to a caste system designed to keep Blacks living as second-class citizens.

We live in a "survival of the fittest" capitalist society, where the top 1 percent of Americans own most of the wealth. This same 1 percent accounts for an overwhelming majority of campaign donations giving them virtual control over the public and private sector. Their right-wing politics reflect a blatant disdain for government welfare, but capitalism doesn't exist without poverty. If you are familiar with economics and the concept of capitalism, you understand that classes matter within the system. The rich and poor are mutually important. Both are needed in order for the system to work. If everyone were wealthy, no blue collar jobs would exist. Who would be left to drive trucks to deliver products to the market? Who would pick up garbage, clean public bathrooms, or serve you at your favorite restaurant?

Our government and economic systems are built to preserve the status quo, keeping the rich thriving and the poor living hand-to-mouth. Our nation's dark history makes this preservation problematic. America became one of the wealthiest nations through the robbing and slaughtering of the indigenous people and subsequent enslaving of Africans by European settlers, creating a dominant race of White Anglo Saxons in America. While we've developed into a more civilized nation, devoid of the widespread enslavement

112

and rampant racial slaughtering, the dominance and privilege of being White remains persistent, with all other races in an inferior political, financial and social position.

The ever-expansive welfare state is proof positive of my allegation. Anyone who has studied finance understands the correlation between education, income, home ownership and seed capital to building wealth. Yet our government would rather spend billions of dollars each year to keep Black people reliant on a biweekly dose of medicine to treat a condition that is curable. Why not invest in the descendants of the people whose blood and sweat helped make this nation great? Why not more subsides toward postsecondary education, homeownership or small businesses? The answer is simple. Because the goal is not financial freedom for Blacks. It is subsidized slavery. If improving the long-term welfare of lower-class citizens was the chief focus, more government funding would be allocated to education—the great equalizer—rather than welfare—the great subsidizer.

Throughout our time living in public housing, my mother and grandmother made efforts to earn and set aside extra funds for a down payment on a property; however, it became increasingly difficult as rent was based on total household income. Any additional earnings would get offset by the increase in rent.

There was a time when our rent exceeded 600 dollars. Still modest by most standards, but when your next door neighbor's rent was only one dollar, it served as a deterrent to work. We saw it as penalizing people who dared to do for themselves.

Genetic Genocide

The future of the Black community lives inside of every young Black woman's womb. The power of a Black woman to usher new life into the world is absolutely unrivaled and critical to the survival of the Black race. With the lingering lack of trust and breakdown in communication between Black men and women pushing both to pursue other options, combined with the high percentage of Black men in prison and Black women declaring independence, the stage has been set for the birth of a new race and death of the Black community.

The threat of the Black community becoming extinct is what single-handily provoked my pen to paper on the topic. To fathom the Black race could survive 400 years of slavery, yet potentially be endangered in the 21st century is beyond comprehension. Nonetheless, we find ourselves at the onset of a modern day ethnic cleansing in the form of genetic genocide.

One afternoon during my daily perusing through social media, I stumbled across a meme that disturbed my spirit and stopped my scroll. You know…the type of post that leaves you sitting in deep thought as the hairs on the back of your neck begin to slowly rise. It read: "Fuck Racism. Have Mixed Babies!" To be fair, I can't be certain what the person who posted it meant by the dare, I can only convey how I received the message. Given that this meme began circulating concurrently with several racially-charged police shootings of unarmed Black men, it reeked of casual racism. More candidly expressed, Black men needed to lighten their skin to reduce the inherent fear caused by their deep melanin. What's more, Black and White people ought to intentionally mate to create a blended society of interracial human beings, to stop the racially-charged killing of minorities, as we'd all be the same.

Beyond the obvious racial insensitivity, what's flawed about this philosophy is that the population of Blacks and Whites in America is not equal. What that post is advocating for is genetic genocide—the death of the Black race as we've known it. Blacks only make up 13 percent of the U.S. population in comparison to Whites who are 62 percent (or roughly 5 times the Black population). Given the disparity in numbers, the Black race would get absorbed much quicker through interracial breeding.

Here is something to consider. You have a hundred cups that are filled with liquid; 13 are Coke, 62 are water and 25 are other. Take 13 waters and combine them with all 13 Cokes, leaving a remainder of 49 waters and 13 Coke-waters (i.e., zero pure Cokes). Take 13 of the remaining 49 waters and combine them with all 13 Coke-water mixtures, leaving 36 pure waters. Finally, take 26 of the remaining 36 pure waters and combine them with the Coke-water-water mixtures. What percentage of Coke is left? You water down a race the same way you water down a Coke, by continuing to dilute the substance until only the remnant is left.

Granted, even one percent of Black blood technically makes you Black by longstanding American standards (e.g., the One-Drop rule or even the anecdotal evidence that most Black-White biracial people are closer to their Black family); however, your interracial blend gives you choices to self-identify: Black, White, interracial, other. When being Black means being subjected to a life of peril and obstacles, when given a choice not many people are willing to pick up their sword and fight.

> "Merely by describing yourself as Black you have started on a road towards emancipation, you have committed yourself to fight against all forces that seek to use your Blackness as a stamp that marks you out as a subservient being." — Steven Biko

From 2000 to 2010, the Black population grew by 12.3 percent while total population growth was 9.7 percent. However, the percent of Blacks combined with Whites (i.e., biracial individuals) grew by 133.7 percent for the same timeframe.

The U.S. Census began collecting data in 1790 but it wasn't until the 2000 census that biracial individuals were provided with their first opportunity to claim more than one race. This allowance subsequently decreased the number of previously Black-alone or White-alone individuals. Some respondents could've been well into their late forties and early fifties, however, statistics suggest that the biracial growth is concentrated in the younger generations. For every hundred Blacks over forty, less than one was identified as both Black and White, compared with more than fifteen out of a hundred Black kids under the age of five. The high density in Black children reflects a clear paradigm shift to a more racially-blended Black community.

I cringe every time I hear a well-intended White person suggest we need a colorblind society. Colorblind is code language for white-washed, carrying a particularly negative connotation for Black

Americans. It's much easier for foreigners to come over to America in search of opportunity and conform to the White Anglo Saxon core culture. Even first-generation Black Africans who come to America will adopt an American name to blend in without batting an eyelash, because their history on American soil is not drenched in blood. However, when those *opportunities* were built on the backs of your ancestors through forced labor, being asked to conform to earn the right to enter into a prosperity you helped create is downright infuriating.

Whether my thoughts toward the meme are accurate or off base, the cultural practice of members of a subordinate sect deliberately mating with members from the dominate sect has been a common occurrence for centuries throughout civilizations across the world.

In East Indian culture, hypergamy, the act of marrying someone of a superior caste or class, can mean the difference between one's daughter living poorly in rural India or having access to better schooling, job opportunities and social status in urban India. As a result, many Indian mother's fixate on the perceived beauty and absolute privilege assigned to fair skin. Daughters are discouraged from playing outside in the summer. They are required to wear high SPF sunscreen year-round. Even skin-bleaching products are used for some darker Indian girls to achieve a desired level of fairness.

Colorism, a prejudice or discrimination against individuals with a dark skin tone (typically among people of the same ethnic or racial group), has created a color hierarchy in many cultures. Not only race but skin tone is helping to shape the life trajectory of individuals. Lighter skin means better treatment and ultimately a

117

better life. Nowhere is it more present than in the Latino culture. In a country like the Dominican Republic where everyone is mixed, (even though the majority of its population is estimated to have African ancestry) race is less significant than skin color.

There is a common phrase in the Dominican Republic "Mejorando La Raza," which means "improve the race." The race is improved by preserving European features (e.g., lighter skin, thin nose, straight hair). Every Dominican child is reared to embrace this ideology. There is immense pressure placed on young men and women to marry people with lighter skin than their own, not only as a cultural responsibility but also for the future of any offspring. Dark-skinned Afro-Dominicans are widely discriminated against— similar to Afro-Cubans, Afro-Mexicans and Afro-Brazilians. Like America, the association of dark skin with criminality is prevalent throughout Latin America. Dark-skinned people are perceived to be prone to violence and portrayed as poor, dirty and dishonest by the mainstream.

Since the colonization of the Americas, the slave trade and subsequent violent raping of African women, Africans throughout the diaspora have been socially divided by skin tone, perpetuating the stereotype that "lighter is righter." Even as a slave, your complexion dictated your quality of life. In the U.S., less melanin landed you a position in the house away from the brutal hardship of the cotton fields. As a result, some Blacks have been conditioned to believe "purifying" the race or lightening the complexion of their offspring, through deliberate interracial mating, is the key to success in our White male dominated society.

By no means am I opposed to interracial dating or marriage. True love has no color limitations, but *motive* matters. The content

118

of a person's character should matter most in pursuing a life partner. If a person's skin is the driving force behind the covenant, the love is not genuine—nor is it enough to sustain a marriage. Genuine love notwithstanding, the impact of interracial Black and White marriages as an act of social acceptance poses a credible threat to the future of Black America.

Equally as alarming as the threat of genetic genocide, are Black population growth trends. College-educated Black women are unlikely to have a child before getting married. In fact, only twelve percent of births by college graduates are to unmarried women.

Meanwhile, working-class Black women (i.e., high school diploma or less) are having children at a much higher rate. Additionally, 83 percent of first births to women without college degrees are to unmarried mothers. This means the lion's share of Black population growth is concentrated in the working class and single mother households. Children in the United States have a 47 percent likelihood of being trapped in the same social class (caste) as their parents—one of the highest rates of any developed country.

With educated Black women delaying childbirth until marriage—risking childlessness—and the birth rates of working-class Black women maintaining speed; if we survive genocide, we will have created a permanent Black underclass.

THE SOLUTION

Imagine a Black community where you're not required to retreat to the suburbs for a safe neighborhood and quality education, often subjecting your children to an environment where few friends look like them. Envision a community where we police ourselves instead of feeling terrorized by corrupt White cops with inherent fear of our darker skin. Imagine, if instead of allowing our culture to be hijacked by vultures, we profited from our likeness. Ponder the thought of a Black community where having an inheritance is as common as owning a pair of Air Jordans.

Picture a fully-independent, thriving Black economy, one that places us in the position of manufacturer or service provider rather than massive consumer. Picture a community where we have the financial capital to fight back against the gentrification, happening right now in many major cities, purchasing land and preserving the property to its incumbents.

All of which are attainable if we can get back to the basics, repairing the relationship and restoring the institution of marriage between Black men and women, as well as changing our views from individual to holistic, by understanding how our decisions impact the whole.

It will require a concerted effort on the part of Black men and women. For many Black men, it means to reciprocate the love Black women have given to us. It means stepping up to the plate and owning our responsibilities. It means overcoming our fear of commitment and uniting with the women who have held us down from the beginning.

For Black women it requires a change in the status quo. The current model is broken. Black women cannot continue to operate in a space that cultivates sovereignty.

The longer the social power struggle exists, the longer Black America will remain powerless against the factors retarding its growth, penniless against gentrification, and defenseless against predatory targeting in disease research or periodic police attacks on the home front. This has been evident recently in Sanford, FL; Cleveland, OH; Staten Island, NY; Ferguson, MO and, of course, in Flint, Michigan, where the entire city's water supply was so polluted it became poison. In every event, no one went to jail for the crimes committed, sending a firm message that Black lives don't matter in this nation. As a community, we must be stronger and more unified! The solidarity we seek starts at home. It starts with the backbone of the Black community; Black women.

Since ultimately, Black women teach Black men how to treat them, there are some general guidelines that Black women could benefit from individually—as change starts within—collectively as Black women and together in relationships with Black men. These guidelines will help increase the dating-to-marriage percentage, subsequently strengthening Black families and the communities we inhabit.

Stop Searching For a Soul Mate

The idea of a soul mate bodes well for the hopeless lover in a romantic comedy, but in reality, believing in a soul mate gives you the false impression you don't have to work on improving yourself. I've found no Biblical evidence supporting the notion that God creates someone specifically for you and only you. The idea that you will meet someone who, by innate design, will embrace all of your flaws without exception is a complete fallacy. No man, and by extension, no relationship will be perfect. We all have to suffer through growing pains as a rite of passage. It's what fortifies our bonds. The sensationalized belief there is a singular somebody in this world made specifically for you keeps many people scouring the earth searching for the other half that makes them whole. All the while, great candidates in plain sight are overlooked.

If you are looking for a "soul mate," it's as simple as finding someone who will risk his life for you and someone worth risking your life for. You will know it's the right person because the timing will be in perfect balance. You won't have to force the issue. Neither of you will need any convincing because you'll both be ready to wholeheartedly embrace love. It will never be the right person without the right timing. To be smitten with someone who is physically or emotionally unavailable is setting yourself up for heartache.

Contrary to popular belief, the loneliest people in the world are not those lacking a significant other. It's those who have found the significance in another, but whose feelings were not returned.

125

Being in love without it being reciprocated is truly a lonely place.

When you find that special love that makes you glow—one that is organic and mutual—bottle and preserve it in your heart. Then guard your heart as if your life depends on it...because it does. When two people come together in marriage their lives grow inseparable, woven together in a distinct quilted pattern. If the two were to separate, it would destroy the beautiful authentic design they've created. Life as they've known it, for however long, would cease to exist. And the construction of a new life pattern would begin. Therefore, be careful who you give your heart to. Don't ask yourself "Is he my soulmate?" Ask yourself "Is he worth dying for?"

Pray For Your Husband

Prayer is a very powerful tool. Those who believe in it and have experienced it at work, recognize its undeniable worth and value. The Word teaches us that faith is "the substance of things hoped for, the evidence of things not seen." If you've reached the point where you're ready to get married, but there are no visible prospects, don't become discouraged. Pray! Take comfort in your prayers. Trust that God knows your heart and He would love nothing more than to send you someone who exceeds your expectations in every way, fulfilling your wants but, more importantly, your needs.

Praying for a mate also helps you become more specific about the qualities you want in a partner. Sometimes we come before the Lord asking for a blessing without a full understanding of what that blessing looks like. So pray in detail, from the superficial physical aspects to the deep-rooted character traits. Prayer is an act of faith. No matter how long it takes, trust that God has not forgotten you.

For those ladies who've consistently prayed and approached dating and relationships in a mature manner, yet always end up hurt, stand on God's promises. "Let us not become weary in doing good, for at the proper time we will reap a harvest if we do not give up." (Galatians 6:9). The "proper" time is once you've been made whole. All your experiences, good or bad, are helping to mold you into the person God designed you to be. Embrace the experiences. Continue to be true to yourself. Don't become jaded. Never allow someone else's wounds to wound you.

> Consider it pure joy, my brothers and sisters, whenever you face trials of many kinds, because you know that the testing of your faith produces perseverance. Let perseverance finish its work so that you may be mature and complete, not lacking anything....Blessed is the one who perseveres under trial because, having stood the test, that person will receive the crown of life that the Lord has promised to those who love him.
>
> James 1:2-4, 12

Prepare For Your Blessing

The old cliché "failing to prepare is preparing to fail" could not be truer regarding marriage. However, I seriously doubt many singles are actively preparing for marriage beyond pre-marital counseling. In theory the preparation process should start before the selection process. It will help you better understand what you need from a mate. The more you define your needs and the more honest you are with yourself, the easier it is to recognize when someone is not a good fit.

It's also important to prepare prior to meeting your potential husband so your house is in order and you are ready to receive your blessing. Getting your house in order might be as practical as repairing your credit. It might consist of taking cooking lessons to get more comfortable in the kitchen. Maybe it's something more involved like volunteering at a food pantry to become more selfless. Cleaning house might be as simple as severing communication with some girlfriends who are bad influences or parting ways with alcohol and other substances that impair your decision making. It all depends on the person.

Dress How You Want to be Addressed

Let me be clear that my advice here is in regards to dating. *Not* rape culture. Suggesting that women invite rape by the way they're dressed is blaming the victims—something I could never stand for. No clothing, or lack thereof, can evoke an action unless the attacker is already prone to such aggression. A woman built like a brick house could walk past me buck naked and nowhere in my mind would I fathom the thought of forcing myself on her. It's the unstable nature of the man, not the way the woman is dressed.

Rape culture notwithstanding, we live in a society full of prejudice. We prejudge based on appearance all the time. The image

128

we present to the world is what we are judged by, and rightfully so. Fashion is a choice. Every day, we make a conscious decision about what to wear. Our clothes are a representation of us. The way we dress should reflect the amount of respect we have and demand for ourselves. It's about maintaining a certain level of decency —which by the way doesn't require wearing all name-brand clothing.

The reality is that people are treated a certain way based on their appearance. Some men will treat all women with respect; most will treat you how you treat yourself. If the way you are dressed suggests you have little respect for yourself, many men won't respect you.

Within seconds of walking into a room, a man will have you placed in a category, with little information other than the way you are dressed and carry yourself: Career Woman v. Gold Digger, Good Girl v. Virgin, Freak v. Slut (Hoe, Bopper, Thot), Dime Piece v. Maybelline Queen, Ride-or-Die v. Crazy. The Career Woman v. Gold Digger comparison acknowledges the difference between a woman whose X5 was paid for without a sponsor. Good Girl v. Virgin is the difference between a lady in the streets who knows how to let her hair down in private and someone who is completely not about it regardless of the environment. Freak v. Slut compares a woman who likes to get kinky only with her man, as opposed to the one who goes all out with every man she meets. Dime Piece v. Maybelline Queen is a woman with natural beauty instead of a woman who is only appealing with makeup. Ride-or-Drive v. Crazy is the difference between a woman who will ride for you opposed to one who will ride down on you!

Ultimately, what a man is trying to figure out is if he should date you, sex you, or leave you the hell alone. If you find that men don't take you seriously, take a good long look in the mirror. Besides family and friends or someone who regularly interacts with you, the rest of the public doesn't have the luxury of knowing who you are on the inside; therefore, you must project your inner-self outward.

Recondition Your Mind

By popular definition, insanity is doing the same thing over and over and expecting a different result. If you desire different results, it requires different actions. However, our actions are merely a reflection of our beliefs, so in essence different results demand a renewed mindset. It may even force you to divorce thoughts about relationships that were passed down to you and develop your own. What you find appealing or who you find attractive may have to change.

You may need to reconsider your definition of love. If you've moved from one physically abusive relationship to the next, maybe you've been conditioned to believe that love is painful. Gentle men with a tender touch turn you off. "No pushovers" is high on your checklist of qualities for a man. Be careful what you wish for. There's a huge difference between a confident man and a caveman. Sometimes a woman will talk out of two sides of her mouth. In one breath, she will say "I just want a man who will treat me right," but that type of guy gets overlooked by the allure of the arrogant. Or (my favorite paradox), when women say they don't want a man who "sweats" them, but the guy they do want is giving them little attention. He's too busy sweating someone else who, in turn, is giving him little attention because she has her eyes set on an altogether different man. And so goes the circle of dating life.

Re-evaluate your checklist. Those hard working gentlemen who've been stuck in the "friend zone" may need to be given thorough reconsideration. Be honest. Are you unequally yoked or is he unacceptably broke? Many good Black men get disqualified because they lack the necessary income to help sustain some women's lifestyles.

Money motivates men for one particular reason over all others: to impress women. If women collectively placed more value on character rather than swagger, perhaps the paradigm would shift. Virtually every decision a man makes directly or indirectly revolves around the perceived desires of a woman. The designer clothes he wears. The luxury car he drives. The penthouse suite he purchased. If character replaced swagger maybe men would spend more money on strengthening their interior instead of spit-shining their exterior. Maybe the focus would be on integrity, self-assessment and breaking bad habits. However, society has conditioned you to desire a bad boy with money and power. You have to decide for yourself what is truly important.

Don't be deceived by the well-dressed zombie or the charming and successful pathological liar. His willingness to spend money on you doesn't mean he loves or respects you. Please see past the superficial and take a deep look at the true essence of the man; the qualities money can't buy. Pay close attention to the way he treats the other women in his life. It will provide you with an honest glimpse into the character of the man. Train your eyes to not ignore the obvious. Train your heart to reject the smooth talking men who will tell you anything to get what they want.

Avoid the narcissist. Independent women often attract overly confident men. Those men who love challenges and desperately need their egos stroked—time and time again. The kind of guy who walks into a room and genuinely believes every woman present is lusting after him. Inherently, if he thinks these women desire him, he will feel inclined to introduce himself to the one he finds most attractive. Consistently opening up that line of communication is not conducive to monogamy.

I'm not suggesting that a man needs to be ready-made. Lord knows I needed fine-tuning. Many Black men will be a little rough around the edges. I'm referring to the men who are rotten down to the core. The cold-hearted men who mean you nothing but harm.

"It's crazy how many times I go to open a door for a Black woman on a date and she races to beat me to the door. Every time their response is 'I'm just used to doing things for myself.' Some act as if I'm being insincere with my politeness, while others react as if I'm insulting them by suggesting they can't open their own door."

—Anonymous

When you've had to strong-arm your way into success like Black women in America, reconditioning the mind also means understanding how to turn on and off that switch. Being an uber aggressive, take-charge, fast-paced Black woman may do well for your career, it won't necessarily help your romantic life. Beyond intimidation, robbing a man of opportunities to pay for a meal, open a door, or simply pick you up for a date are examples of micro-emasculation. Over time these subtle yet impactful transgressions can erode the foundation of a relationship causing it to collapse.

Black women have to learn to develop split personalities, one reserved for conducting business and another for intimate relationships. As a former college football player, I'm remarkably familiar with this concept. Football is an extremely violent sport. In order to play the game at a high level you have to match the game's intensity. You have to be angry, at times aggressive and reckless. If I'd taken the same attitude off the field with me, it would've been a recipe for disaster. I had to learn how to turn it on and off, because what made me successful in the football arena would have made me a criminal outside of it. Black women must understand that their take-charge attitude in Corporate America can be toxic when it spills over into their personal life.

Get Checked for SCS (Side-Chick Syndrome)

There is way too much friendly fire in this sisterhood of divine divas. Side chicks have become as abundant as weeds in a flower garden—and just as unwanted. They swoop in and play the role of superwoman satisfying the 20 percent of whatever is lacking at home, but fail to possess strong enough qualities to sustain the other 80 percent to assume the main role.

Truthfully, some men lie, shockingly enough, so determining if you are a side-chick might not be as obvious. SCS is in reference to women who knowingly enter into relationships with men who

133

are off limits. Schedule an appointment with a friend or a trusted confidant. Together, work through your history of recent relationships. If any or all of the men in your past had a significant other before, (which you interfered with) or during the relationship, you are likely suffering from side-chick syndrome. It's a continuum with four levels ranging from the grade one "slightly" to the grade four "completely."

It's understood that statistically there are just not enough Black men to go around, so some Black women feel sharing someone else's man is the only way to have one. Or continuing with the New-Age feminist thought, these ladies are not side chicks or mistresses; they are simply modern women—free to move around like men. It's all fun and games as long as you're seated in the side chick position, but when the chicken comes home to roost and you find yourself in the shoes of the main woman, sharing becomes much more sobering.

I don't care who he is or what he's worth. Don't allow yourself to settle for the proverbial "side chick" status. Having your condo paid for by a professional athlete who is married is not impressive it's oppressive. The expectation is that you're supposed to be home when he has a break in his schedule and wants to swing by and sex you. You will never be anything more than a break in the monotony, someone to have fun with on occasions. You will never be the person in the light. Your life will consist of darkness and silence, unable to be seen in public and unable to acknowledge you even know the person.

The psychological effects of living in secrecy and hiding in shadows damages your self-esteem. It sends a message to your brain that says, "I'm not good enough." Being a side chick, on the surface, may seem to have its benefits providing you with money, cars, jewelry and

134

vacations without the responsibilities and restrictions. But inevitably you will grow tired of waiting in the wings and will want your shot in the primary seat.

Learn Code Language

It's difficult to determine the motive of every man who approaches you. Always assuming the worst would make you a cynic; however, believing every word a man says would make you gullible. Men lie, as do women. Learning to decipher code language, verbal and non-verbal, can be the difference in giving your heart to the wrong man or eliminating him as a viable candidate.

If a man tells you that he doesn't believe in labels. He's almost certainly lying. By nature, men are territorial creatures. Since childhood, we've used labels to mark the territory of items we value. If we went to shoot hoops in the park and brought our favorite basketball, it most certainly had our name or initials somewhere on it. We wanted to make sure everyone knew this was our ball. Labeling someone as our girlfriend is no different. A man's unwillingness to claim you is a blatant lack of commitment. It's not that he doesn't believe in labels. He just doesn't believe in labeling you, specifically, as his woman. He wants the ability to move freely without the burden of a relationship. He's likely prone to disappearing acts, or only hanging out with you during the week and not the weekend. It's because you're not his primary love interest.

If not even his pinky toe touches you after sex, he is likely using you only for sex. Obviously, not all men are inclined to cuddle, but a drastic change in his demeanor is a dead giveaway. Many men have

135

experienced the instantaneous feeling of disgust, post-ejaculation, when lying with a woman they're only entertaining for sex. If you only hang-in and never hangout, as in a date, that's another dead giveaway. If you used to go on dates prior to having sex, and now he only comes over to visit, it's his way of recouping the overhead cost of the start-up of sex. Like a business, he's looking for the return on his investment.

It's a thin line between secrecy and privacy, but there is a differ-ence. A private person is guarded and doesn't offer up any informa-tion above and beyond what is asked. Sharing makes them uncom-fortable. It's a threat to their security. However, a secretive person is attempting to conceal information. Their actions are conscious. A consistently facedown phone (or one that is always in airplane mode) is absolutely cause for concern. It's a conscious decision he is making to conceal some sort of extracurricular activity. Maybe it's not another woman; maybe it's a Ponzi Scheme, either way it should make you suspicious. Keep in mind, suspicion is not a basis for the invasion of privacy. Snooping around will break down the trust in a relationship. If trust is already compromised, you have to question if finding proof is even necessary. Most of the time when a woman is desperately searching for a smoking gun, it's an ongoing excuse not to end the relationship. Even when the elusive hardcore evidence is found, these women figure out how to explain away the issue. It's never about the evidence. It's about coming to grips with the loss of a relationship without denying yourself the ability to celebrate all that was once enjoyable about it.

Beware of the man with the wandering eye. Unless it's a doc-umented medical condition, it reflects an obvious lack of respect for you and other women—depending on where he is looking. If a man can't refrain from looking at other women in your presence, imagine how he behaves in your absence. Granted, being in a committed relationship doesn't turn a man gay. He is still attracted to the opposite sex. But it's about discipline. If he can't train his eyes to look and then look away, it's likely a sign of a deeper rooted problem. There are plenty of warning signs. Don't dismiss this offense as a "man being a man" because it's socially accepted and not a more egregious infraction. Eyes are where it all begins. First you see an image. Next you desire it. "Then, after desire has conceived, it gives birth to sin; and sin, when it is full-grown, gives birth to death." (James 1:15).

Inflexibility is common code language for lack of interest. If a man has a "my way or the highway" attitude, it's because he has no fear of losing you. Either he's apathetic towards the relationship or he's convinced that you can't find anyone better. Don't ever let a man make you feel like you should be lucky he's giving you an opportunity. He will not respect you. He will talk down to you and treat you like you're expendable. Love yourself enough to demand more from a relationship, even if he is the richest man this side of the Atlantic Ocean.

If a man asks, "Do you know how many women would love to…" fill in the blank, it's a power play. It's likely because you are resisting in some area. His goal is to make you expendable and him irreplaceable. If he can convince you that you're a dime a dozen, he wins!

First impressions are important. If a man shows you his true colors believe him the first time. If a man tries to sleep with you on the first date, it's not simply because he is horny, it's because he's not looking for anything deeper from you. Not every guy who tries to sleep with you has bad intentions. He might just be misguided. Some guys have a sense of entitlement and believe sex comes with the territory. But beware, men with entitlement issues are more likely to stray.

If he invites you on a dinner date and doesn't offer to pay the bill, he doesn't believe in chivalry and you will feel the effects of it in other areas. If he is habitually late, it's because you're not a priority, you're an option.

If he's in a relationship, yet aggressively pursuing you, don't believe he is acting out of character or that he is going through all this trouble because you're "so special." He will sell you one sweet lie after another. As a loyal woman, you'll believe in your heart a truth that fails to convince your mind. Then time after time, heartbreak after heartbreak, you'll grow jaded, finally coming to the realization he's not worthy of your time. These same immature men get recycled back into the dating pool to do more harm to other women giving the false impression of a higher percentage of deceitful Black men. Beware!

Unmask, Unsew and Unglue

As a man, I realize I will never fully understand women. However, I believe that beyond self-fulfillment, single Black women want to look attractive to potential dating candidates. In that vein, I do know what Black men prefer. While I won't generalize and propose we are a monolithic group with standard beliefs about beauty, there is a common perspective shared among us. We are convinced Black women don't like the way they naturally look. Not their face or natural melanin. Not their hair…nothing! The natural movement notwithstanding, the majority of Black women look in the mirror and see a self-image rather than a reflection. Best articulated by Israel Houghton in his "Name of Love" lyrics "The type of hair, the clothes she wears reflects the way she feels about herself compared to someone else." Since when did Black women begin measuring their beauty in terms of artificial products rather than natural features? When did your voluptuousness need augmentation by injections?

I'm not suggesting that every Black woman should walk around looking like mother of the earth. It's not about forcing Black women into a box and creating a homogenous look. A natural style might not appeal to everyone. Regardless, hair manufacturers have even found a way to make the natural look unnatural with synthetic kinky hair. There is nothing necessarily unbecoming about wearing hair weaves or makeup individually. It's the totality of it all that becomes problematic.

As a young child, I can remember my first time seeing RuPaul on television. I said, "She looks scary!" It wasn't until my mother explained that "she" was actually a "he" that I gained clarity. RuPaul was a drag queen, a man who dressed in women's clothing. Before the days of hormone pills and gender reassignment surgery, if a man desired to look like a woman he had to dress in drag or cross-dress. There were many styles and ways in which drag queens dressed from Burlesque to gothic. However, what they all had in common was embellishment. This typically consisted of over-the-top makeup, skimpy clothing and long flowing wigs and weaves— not to mention long eyelashes and fingernails. Every aspect of their

139

appearance was exaggerated.

Fast forward to present day, when I see Black women scanti-ly clad with excessive makeup, unbelievably long eyelashes and an overblown weave, I immediately question her gender—especially if she has a masculine facial structure. In this new transgender age, the last inner debate you want a man to engage in is whether or not you are a woman. To that end, I suggest that Black women unmask their faces, unsew their weaves, unglue their eyelashes and unlock the true natural beauty within them. Unmasking is not about con-forming; it's about being comfortable in one's own skin.

In 2015, singer Alicia Keys decided to unmask her face and em-brace the no-makeup look. I've always viewed Alicia as a naturally gorgeous woman. Never could I imagine her struggling to bare her naked face. Yet here was a woman, idolized by many young wom-en, suffering from her own powdered self-image. Hearing her dis-cuss her insecurities, from childhood to stardom, reminded me just how deeply wounded we can be by the judgmental world around us.

I've heard the argument from several Black women that weaves are versatile and easy to maintain for reasons why they wear them. Versatility I can respect. However, conventional wisdom teaches us that the easiest solution is not always the best solution. Also, based on the excessive amount of tacky weaves I've seen, I would argue that the amount of maintenance required is either misunderstood or underestimated. I used to believe it was a socioeconomic prob-lem with lower-class Black women unable to afford top-dollar hair or leaving their weaves in too long, but after further review the problem seems rampant, transcending all social classes.

When I see Black women who normally wear weaves rock their

natural hair I'm almost always astounded that they wouldn't do it more often. I feel like I'm living out a scene from the early nineties movie *Pretty Woman* when Julia Roberts was a prostitute. She wakes up in the morning from an overnight stay with her client, Richard Gere, and he discovers that the blonde wig is not her real hair. Underneath it is this gorgeous, curly red hair that she's been hiding. Gere is dumbfounded, as am I wondering why on earth Black women would pay to have someone cover up their natural beauty. The weave cheapens them. It looks unnatural. Often the color doesn't match their skin tone. The super long hair gets tangled and matted or the super glossy weave makes their hair look greasy.

However, most troubling is a recent study by Johns Hopkins Medicine that found a "strong association" between weaves, braids and hair extensions to permanent hair loss. Researchers argue that these hairstyles have a tendency to pull on the scalp and contribute to the development of traction alopecia, a condition an estimated one-third of Black women suffer from.

While weaves are supposedly "low maintenance," makeup is the complete opposite. It requires an extra hour to get ready in the morning or evening—not to mention the time it requires to remove it at night. Some women elect to wear the same makeup the next day giving a new meaning to the expression "saving face."

There is nothing easy about wearing makeup. It takes patience and a certain level of skill to master a smoldering smokey eye or the perfect pouty lips. Men in general appreciate a woman who takes pride in her appearance. However, when it comes to makeup… less is more. It shouldn't be a 12-step process. It's makeup, not rehab.

A woman's face should match the rest of her body's skin tone. Accentuating your features shouldn't be invasive or necessitate shaving your eyebrows then repositioning them with an eyebrow pencil. Makeup is supposed to enhance your beauty not detract from it, nor should it be worn so often that you feel naked without it. When you remove the layers of powder, mascara, eyeliner, eye shadow, bronzer and blush what you will often find is a flawed foundation built on superficial beauty and marred with hidden insecurities.

> Your beauty should not come from outward adornment, such as elaborate hairstyles and wearing of gold jewelry or fine clothes. Rather, it should be that of your inner self, the unfading beauty of a gentle and quiet spirit, which is of great worth in God's sight.
>
> 1 Peter 3:3-4

Get Serious Sooner

When I pose the question, "When did you begin dating seriously?" to single Black women in their thirties the answer is consistently, "Late twenties." Becoming serious that late in the game doesn't afford much margin for error—especially if you want children.

Taking a more serious approach to dating sooner doesn't necessarily mean marrying young. It also doesn't mean crossing into your thirties and becoming Agent 007 on operation "Get Hitched Quick." It means don't waste time "dating just to date." If there is no potential in the man don't date him. If there is no potential for a serious relationship don't enter into a casual one. Scrutinize every man under the marriage-material lens. If you know in your mind that you could never marry him, don't waste time in a dead-end relationship.

Getting serious sooner will help you grow personally; honing your skills and zeroing in on the qualities you seek in a husband. Surround yourself with women who are happily married, in healthy relationships, or who at least *like* men. Women who only man bash will negatively influence your own outlook and outcome.

The unfortunate reality is that time is on his side...not yours. He can waste away his entire twenties "sowing his royal oats" and still recover in his thirties or rebound in his forties. Black women (or women in general) don't have the same luxury. You can take a "power position" and sex men for fun, proving to the world that men aren't the only ones entitled to explore their sexuality, but there are two major forces working against you in the form of a biological clock and competition.

While advancements in medical technology have helped to extend the window for child bearing, age remains the largest factor in fertility. Women who wait, put their health, the health of their baby, and the odds of conception at major risk.

Fertility is at its highest in your twenties. Still the rate of women under twenty-five experiencing problems conceiving has significantly increased. Waiting until your thirties only magnifies the issue. Ovaries have a defined life expectancy. Every year the number of usable (mature) eggs declines until you run out. Ovulation is uncommon if the eggs are immature and the odds of fertilization become virtually nonexistent—not to suggest that it couldn't happen through some divine intervention.

Don't delay pursuing a family for your career. Do it simultaneously. Leanne and I married at twenty-three and twenty-five respectively. At the time, it felt extremely young to tie the knot. But fast forward nine years and three kids to present day, both of us now in our thirties and we're glad we didn't wait. For one, as it relates to children, I don't think either of us would have the energy in our forties to chase around three kids five and under. Secondly, contrary to popular belief, marriage didn't hinder our success it propelled it. Having that void filled in our lives was liberating. It provided a peace of mind that allowed us to channel our efforts towards building wealth, both tangible and intangible, instead of stressing over our love lives. Working in tandem we've been able to accomplish more as a team than we ever would have as individuals.

The other looming concern which has reaffirmed my belief about Black women getting serious sooner is competition. A Black woman in her mid-thirties looking to date a Black man in his mid-thirties is not only competing with other women in her age bracket, but also Black women ten to fifteen years her junior. I truly believe this aspect gets overlooked more than any when examining Black women's marital rates. It's already been established that the pool of available Black men has decreased. The remaining single Black men have a wide variety of Black women to choose from.

Black women are typically confined to dating men within their age range or older—which is mostly their preference. Whereas a Black man's options are completely open. In general, a forty-year-old Black woman will only be able to reach down as far as thirty to date a younger man. However, a forty- year-old man can reach down as far as twenty to find a mate. Her young eggs also serve as his fountain of youth, giving him the ability to have children at an older age.

The stiff competition in the Black dating market suggests women who wait to get married significantly lessen their chances of getting married to a man who has no kids and has never been married before. If experiencing marriage and childbirth for the first time with your mate are important to you, get serious about dating sooner.

Keep Your Options Open

There are no guarantees in dating. Sometimes you hit a home run. Sometimes you strike out. However, you increase your odds of winning with your approach and more opportunities, which is why I suggest keeping your options open. Too many young Black women are exhausting their youth tied down to the wrong man. They have the right type of loyalty to the wrong type of guy. You give him the best five years of your twenties. In return, he gives you a baby with no strings attached. Not only has he robbed you of your youth, but he's also made you less desirable in the dating market. Finding a husband is much harder as a single-mother than a single woman.

Part of the problem stems from a lack of maturity that only comes with age. *Dating* is not a recognized marital status—under law or in the eyes of God. It's a precursor to marriage. It's a tool designed to help bring your ideal spouse into focus. Therefore, don't put all your eggs in one basket. Make him earn the right to be the only man in your life. Don't just give him that luxury. If he's not willing to step up to the challenge then explore other options. I'm not suggesting you sleep around. I'm suggesting you date around. There is a difference. Contrary to popular belief, dating and sex are not synonymous.

Exploring your options also doesn't mean you become a player with a heavy rotation of men—long term. If you're getting serious sooner, then you will constantly be evaluating each situation to determine which man deserves your undivided attention.

The average age of first marriage in the U.S. is twenty-seven for women, up from twenty-three in 1990. As women are getting married later, some are not getting married at all. If I'm a Black woman and I'm between the ages of twenty-five and thirty, I'm making any man who wishes to be my boyfriend prove that he is serious and capable of a monogamous relationship. He'll have to do more than send flowers and heart-eyes emojis to profess his love. Why? Because those critical dating years will determine if you will marry and to whom.

Never Put a Price Tag on Your Cookie

We live in a superficial world; from plastic surgery to material possessions. Everything is on the surface. Who are you wearing?

146

What kind of car do you drive? How much money do you make? I take no exception to people wanting the "finer things" in life; however I find fault in those seeking it by any means necessary, "For what is a man profited, if he shall gain the whole world, and lose his own soul?" (Matthew 16:26). To lose your soul, in the non-Biblical sense means once you've attained your goal, you can't look yourself in the mirror. You have lost your sense of self-purpose, morals and dignity.

In the Black community, being a professional football or basketball player is perceived as the zenith of success. Athletes are idolized and celebrated more than any other profession. The cumulative effect of being young, rich and famous makes Black professional athletes hot commodities in the dating market. With reality series showcasing ex-girlfriends and ex-wives of these athletes, the desire to snag a baller has reached an all-time high.

Being a former Division 1 athlete with several friends and former teammates who currently play or have played in the NBA and NFL, I've been privy to an inner-circle that eludes most. I've seen the late night foolery in the VIP room and at the annual invite-only mansion pool parties. I've had exclusive access to nightclubs in the arenas and a backstage pass to a life of luxury that some would give their first born to experience... and they do. The amount of opportunistic women, otherwise known as "groupies" and "gold diggers," mixed into the crowd of players' wives hoping for the chance to land a rich baby daddy is mind-boggling. Some are rookies in the game, others are career side chicks. The lengths to which these women will travel to stay on the payroll and remain a part of the inner-circle is scary. Even in the face of complete and utter disrespect, they swallow what is left of their tattered ego and fall in line.

Desire a pedestal instead of a trophy case. Society encourages women to think and feel like a commodity, keeping relationships purely transactional. But if you have a price you can easily be used and discarded after the purchase. Avoid entering into a barter relationship where he shares his dough for a piece of your cookie. Selling your cookie to the highest bidder will never produce profit. His dough will never outweigh your cookie, no matter how rich, unless you put a price tag on it. Dough can be shared without giving it all. Cookie is either all or nothing. He can share his dough and make more. You have one cookie. Once it's compromised, there are no reserves.

Preserve your cookie. Keep it fresh. No matter how many buyers are in the market for your unique blend, *never* sell yourself. What you possess is priceless, like a promise from God. Would you ever consider auctioning off a promise God specifically entrusted to you? Of course not. You would guard that promise and protect it accordingly. You would understand that you were blessed so you may be a blessing and share your promise with only those deserving of it.

If it's in God's plan for you to be rich, you will never have to sacrifice your morals to make it happen. Don't be so desperate for fame or fortune that you're willing to do anything to achieve it. Don't look at people who are behaving unethically, yet appear to be prospering, as blessed. Money can be a gift or a curse. It has ruined many people's lives. Money itself does not cause harm; it's the mindset of the people chasing the money that dictates how money will impact their lives.

The Bible says "It is easier for a camel to go through the eye of

148

a needle, than for a rich man to enter the kingdom of God." (Matthew 19:24). The 21st century urban translation of that scripture reads, "With money like Puffy or a body like Buffie [the Body], it is almost impossible to live righteously." God loves the rich and the poor alike. But he understands the power of money in our society and the difficulty of living upright with that power.

In my New-Age version, I included women and their bodies because unlike men, their power mainly derives from their hips rather than their pocketbooks. A beautiful woman with an hourglass shape can use her physical beauty as power to gain whatever she wants or needs, developing relationships for the sole purpose of monetary gain. We see these types of women every day in our society, folks who appear to be getting ahead on their good looks alone.

There is a great deal of women, many on social media, projecting glamorous lives who are secretly dying inside. Their pictures, followers and likes will have you envious of a person who is on the verge of suicide. Neither beauty nor money can substitute happiness. Some of the prettiest and wealthiest people are severely depressed. At times, the world can seem unbearable; however, you have to keep life in proper perspective. It's never as bad or as good as you think. Choose happiness despite your circumstances. Surround yourself with positivity, and most importantly, don't evaluate your success by someone else's scale of measurement. Don't compare yourself with a woman who puts a price tag on her cookie, seeing all that she has gained and ignoring all that she has given up, thinking that she's winning and you're losing.

149

Step Outside Your Circle

If you're ever in Chicago on a Sunday during the summer (which I highly suggest), drive through the south side. Make your way down State until you reach 47th Street. You will know you have arrived if on your right side there is a sea of Black people, a co-ed flag football league which at its peak housed over 45 teams. A twenty-five player roster equates to over a thousand young Black business professionals (mainly) coming together every weekend. Men running around shirtless or in fitted Under Armour Combat gear, some women wearing sports bras and Spandex, others in kitten heels and summer dresses.

An all-day affair, it is as much a social event as it is recreational, equipped with as much barbecue and booze as sweat and grass stains. Standard procedure is to come early for warm-ups and walk-throughs before your game. Then stick around to socialize over jerk chicken and Jell-O shots.

It started with my wife and me both playing in the league. When we had our first child, it was just me. I played off and on for a couple more teams, until ultimately I decided to hang up my cleats. It was a tough decision. I enjoyed the competition, but Sunday games were interfering with my spiritual development. Plus, the sideshow was starting to overshadow the main event. Herding too much estrogen and testosterone together in a confined space, with little boundaries within the park's gates was a recipe for disaster.

I've seen tears on the field from broken bones to broken hearts. The league has all the makings of a soap opera. She's

150

dating him, but he's sleeping with her etcetera…etcetera. Like the time I disappeared for a year and a half, after the birth of my son, only to return and learn a woman who had given birth to a son and married the father—and quarterback of her team—was now on the team of another quarterback in the same league—literally and figuratively.

Recycling yourself through the same circle of men is never a good look. Few men want someone's sloppy seconds. As said before, all men are territorial creatures. We like to pretend we're the only sex partner you've ever had. However, that fantasy gets quickly ruined by the reality that you've slept with three other men in the same flag league or half the players on your college's football team.

Step outside your immediate circle. Institute a rule that you won't date anyone who has dated your friends. Get out and travel. See what other type of men other cities have to offer. There are statistics that suggest your chances for love is largely linked to your city. Depending on your city's dating statistics, a relocation may just be what the doctor ordered. If you're not brave enough to uproot to a new city, at least be adventurous enough to explore online dating. Though be aware of often misleading online profiles and once you've "met" someone with potential online, invest in the time to get to know them. I'm an advocate for creating opportunities. If you're someone who lives a very routine life of work-home-sleep-repeat, there isn't much opportunity for romance. In this case, the Internet can be your best friend, because it travels faster and further than your car, opening up your pool of prospects.

If you only date men within your circle of friends, social

groups, or geographic location, then you'll be predisposed to a specific type of man. But if you are seeking greatness you may have to venture off the reservation. Greatness knows no boundaries. It only recognizes its likeness in another.

Stay Out of the Driver's Seat

When I met Leanne, I was seeing other women, all of whom had received some version of why I wasn't interested in pursuing a deeper relationship with them. Then suddenly, within weeks of hanging out with Leanne, they all received the same contradicting—and undoubtedly annoying—phone call that I was severing ties with them to pursue a serious relationship with someone else. Talk about a blow to the ego. It's human nature for any woman in that situation to ask the question "Why wasn't I good enough?" But it's not a reflection of you. It's a reflection of his feelings toward you.

If a man is not genuinely interested in you, there is no length you can travel to change his mind. I was friends with a woman who would dog-sit for me when I was out of town. At the time I didn't own a car. Not only would she pick up my dog from my apartment, she would take my dirty laundry with her. When I'd fly back into town, my groomed dog and basket full of folded laundry would be delivered to my doorstep. I considered the woman a good friend; however, we had crossed the line of physical contact in our friendship, which had me worried that these thoughtful acts were not without purpose.

152

If she was truly helping me out of the kindness of her heart, from one friend to another, I was extremely grateful for her support. However, I believed she had an ulterior motive, attempting to prove she was girlfriend material. But there was never any doubt about her ability to love me. I questioned my ability to love her. She was missing the "It" factor. I knew this because whenever I considered a relationship, I had to list off all of her great qualities in an attempt to convince myself to pull the trigger. Maybe I suffer from a romanticized view of love, but I don't believe a relationship is something you should have to force. It should happen organically.

The key to a courtship that ultimately leads to marriage—rests on the man being more interested than the woman—especially in the Black dating community. The lack of available Black men has some Black women going from zero to a hundred… real quick! With all due respect to the Danica Patricks of the world, don't fight for pole position. Rushing will only make you look thirsty and scare off men with commitment issues. You'll find yourself in a relationship headed nowhere fast!

Obviously, there must be shared interest by the woman; however, his must supersede hers. That doesn't mean a woman should assume a nonchalant posture, fronting like she has no feelings for a man. That's the quickest way to get dumped. It means in a traditional courtship, one in which the man is the pursuer, he will make the first move by introducing himself. Men like to pursue. Women who make the mistake of approaching a man first fail to understand the way men's minds work. Can a butterfly be caught that landed in your hand? Can a soldier be captured who waved the white flag? Hand delivering yourself into the arms of a man

153

destroys the excitement and diminishes the pursuit. Not to mention, the blatant disregard of a social norm makes you seem desperate, which is never attractive.

If a woman is interested, she can send subtle non-verbal cues
to let a man know he would be successful in his pursuit. They
exchange information. Then, the man is required to make initial
contact if he would like to invite her on a date. Every step of the
way he is required to lead the interaction, from sending "thinking
of you" flowers to asking to officially enter into a monogamous relationship. He has to constantly pursue her love, ultimately asking
for her hand in marriage—even then the pursuit has to continue...

Men and women are very different. Women have an uncanny
ability to grow to love that most men don't possess. In fact, for a lot
of men it's the opposite; they suffer from relationship A.D.D. and
get bored quickly. A man may start off full throttle with his foot to
the floor coming after you, but often it's not sustainable. He will
ease off the gas. It's just a question of "how much?" If he's feeling
you the slowdown will be slight and gradual with him maintaining
moderate to high speed. However, if he's bored his departure will
be so abrupt, it will feel like a rug was pulled out from under you.
All is fair in love and war. There are no guarantees. But staying
out of the driver's seat will to some degree insulate you from Black
male commitment issues.

Set the Rules Of Engagement

For the life of me I cannot understand why women place restraints on themselves when dating. You may not be able to control the speed at which a relationship progresses, but you most certainly can set the course. That means, though you can't rush a man into a monogamous relationship, you can ensure the relationship remains platonic.

By choosing to remain platonic, you are setting a forward trajectory. He understands you're not interested in a casual relationship or being friends with benefits. You are looking to build with someone, so if the relationship is going to grow into something more significant, you require far more from him. That's how you dictate the course. Too many young ladies are giving more and demanding less when truthfully you should be giving less and demanding more. The ball is always in your court. Never forget that. Don't settle for friends with benefits if you truly want a relationship.

As a kid growing up, I lived on the basketball court. We played open-ended from sun up until a bully showed up. He would come and change the rules of the game, cheating and flexing his power every step of the way. The only option at that point was to take the ball and go home—a passive-aggressive way to control the situation. The look on the bully's face as I turned to walk away was priceless, poetic justice for interrupting our basketball bliss.

When it comes to dating, Black women need to adopt the same practice. Set the rules of engagement. Don't assume a man inherently knows how to treat you (or treat women in general).

Establish parameters. If you're not interested in a texting relationship, don't allow one.

In a text-happy era, where young men can simply text a young woman WTMD and get a positive response, boundaries are absolutely necessary. WTMD is an abbreviation for What That Mouth Do? an inquiry into how adept a girl is at oral sex? Inherently, if he's asking it's because he has yet to experience it. Since when has "good head" become an acceptable prescreening question for dating? What happened to "Did you go to college?" or "Do you believe in God?" What's worse is there are misguided young women, evidently with low self-worth, who actually find this brand of sexism appealing—instead of appalling. This line of questioning shouldn't even be dignified with a response.

All women are different. Some women demand more—time, attention, structure—than others. Some women accept having a part-time lover. You have to approach the situation as if the last person the man dated was your complete opposite—polar idiosyncratic. For instance, some Black women are more traditional and expect a gentleman to pick her up for all dates, other Black women will literally pull a knife on you if you show up at her house for a first date.

You must lay down the ground rules and remain true to them. Don't stay silent in situations where his actions warrant reproach. Silence equals consent. Consent implies permission. Don't give a man permission to walk all over you. Don't let the fear of being alone overpower your sense of self-worth. No "good morning" text or affectionate kiss is more important. Know your value.

Don't be under the false impression that asking questions will scare a man away. If he leaves it's because he's not ready for anything serious. There is a huge difference between nagging, and gaining a clear understanding. If the direction of the relationship is uncertain, you are well within your rights to ask as many questions as necessary. After all, you're sacrificing time and energy that could be invested elsewhere.

Don't sacrifice your happiness for the sake of his. Don't give him what he wants if you're not getting the same in return. He wants time together and likely intimacy. You want answers. No answers. No time. You would be surprised at how fast the tables can turn once you start asserting your authority. Overnight, you go from sweating him to vice versa, as momentum swings to your side. When the rules of the game change, you don't have to stay and play by his rules. You can simply take your ball and leave—and you should!

Those who struggle with this approach also struggle with letting go. You have to become an expert at escorting men to the door when they don't belong in your space. You have to embrace the beauty in moving on. If you believe that by moving on you're missing out, you will fight to hold on to a man who's not worth your energy. Sometimes you will groom a man for his next relationship, but that's perfectly all right. As long as you keep moving forward without dwelling on the past, your future is guaranteed to be better. That means no calling or texting to see how he's doing or stalking him, or his new boo, on social media. Be satisfied knowing that you are both better off apart.

If you set the proper parameters, you'll weed out all the imposters. Initially, many men might show strong interest. They might give you much attention and wait on you hand-and-foot, but only the real men with real interest will be able to withstand the test of time.

Find a Guy with the Right Type of Pride

So many young Black men are growing up in households without fathers, making it difficult for them to learn how to treat a woman, or what it means to be a man. In the absence of fathers, they are forced to learn what it means to be a man on their own, which is influenced by what they see around them. Raised in the streets of the south side of Chicago, I was nurtured to believe "All women are hoes!" not by my mother, but by the streets that raised me.

I was taught "the game" at a very young age. If you stood on the block long enough, you were bound to come across some older father-like figure eager to drop some knowledge on the younger generation.

"Listen up young bloods, I'm only gon' say it once. All women are hoes! That includes yo' mama, my mama and any other mama out there. It's all a game. Once you figure that out, use it to your advantage. Bitches try to use their pussy as power over us. But don't let 'em. These weak niggas be out here trickin', paying for these bitches. But a nigga like me never pay for it. I use my mouthpiece. That's all I need. I ain't buying a bitch bubble gum even if her breath stinks."

The game made reference to the adversarial relationship between Black men and women. The idea is that ultimately men use women for sex and women in turn use men for money. The object of the game is to figure out how to get what you want without giving up something in return. The men who are good at accomplishing this goal were considered to have "game" or a "mouthpiece" and are referred to as players or pimps. The difference between the two is that a pimp exploits their subject for the sole purpose of making money, while a player does it simply for the love of the game.

As a guy, if you considered yourself a player, you had to have at least five women on your "team." You needed an all-star, someone who gets all the fame and fortune, which is usually a guard. Then you needed a support player, someone to help assist the all-star. You needed a couple of role players to fulfill the less glamorous roles. Last but not least, you had your post player, the one you were going hard in the paint on.

The game was said to be "sold not told," because understanding the rules put you at a competitive advantage over your peers (same sex) and gave you leverage over the opponent (the opposite sex). If someone "kicked knowledge" to you about the game, it was like you just received insider trading tips. You treated it like G14 classified information. There were too many rules to the game to explain, but the long and short of it all was "Don't trust women."

As a kid, I rejected these misogynistic views of women. Being raised by my mother and grandmother, I had a healthy outlook on women. That would change with three short words in the summer of '95, "I'm moving out."

After ending a long-term relationship with my father, my

mother began dating a gentleman she met through a co-worker. He liked to party and have fun, a refreshing change from my father who never wanted to go anywhere or do anything. She had been a mother since she was twenty-one years old. She never had the chance to be young and have fun. The previous 14 years of her life revolved around work and her children. She was tired. For the first time in many years she was enjoying her youth, so she decided to put herself first for once and move in with her boyfriend. That decision would put a strain on our relationship for years to come.

My mother was the first woman to ever break my heart. As her youngest child, we formed a special bond. To others, my mother was probably just some poor young Black girl living in the projects with her three kids, but to me she was the Queen of the Nile. I adored her. When another man came along and broke our bond, the pain I felt made me bitter. I knew no matter how strong the feelings my mother's new boyfriend had for her, they paled in comparison to my love…so "Why would she leave me?"

I found myself embracing the words from the old heads on the block. Girls became nothing more than a sport akin to catch-and-release fishing. I never saw myself as a womanizer. I was a competitor; so once "gettin' women" became a game, I wanted to be the best at it. I had a steady girlfriend, from time-to-time, but that never stopped me from playing the field. I was a football player, so the field was my natural habitat.

The more success I had on the football field, the more appealing I was to the ladies. It seemed with every touchdown, I became more and more attractive. I had managed to remain relatively humble throughout all the success, but all the attention started to take its toll. Eventually, my strong confidence developed into a cocky swagger…or what my granny referred to as "The Football Boy Strut."

I was a self-proclaimed "go getta'," meaning if a beautiful girl stepped in the room, I had to go get her. I was aggressive with my agenda and I surrounded myself with like-minded predators. All of us were raised by single mothers and older sisters who we cared about dearly, but you learn to separate the women of your family from all the other women in the world. This helped you to not care, or make the connection that these girls were somebody's daughter, sister or cousin. We even mocked men who befriended women without a sexual agenda.

"Heard you and Melanie went to the show Friday."
"Yeah we did."
"Heard you picked her up, paid for the tickets and bought her popcorn."
"Yeah so."
"Lame ass nigga. What you get it return? You hit?"
"Naw it ain't even like that."
"I guess trick or treatin' came early this year."

It took me moving from my environment and undergoing a deep reconditioning in college to change my sexist thoughts. I was able to rediscover my true essence and not simply be a product of my childhood environment. I opened my Bible and found the value in being a good man.

The good news is that Black men have a natural tendency to

161

be proud. We all take pride in the areas we deem important; however, we all place value in different areas. If a man prides himself on being a great dad, he will make every effort to be present for his children. Some men take pride in their ability to provide. They puff up their chests and stroll into the corporate world wearing their "provider" badge of honor. Some men take pride in their car. They wash and wax their car every other day, despite rain being in the forecast. Others take pride in their physical appearance, spending countless hours in the gym or thousands of dollars on the latest fashions.

On the other hand, some men lean toward more destructive behavior. They take pride in simply making pretty babies with no plans of helping raise them. If a man fancies himself a pimp, he will take pride in his ability to manipulate women. He will take her trust for granted and abuse it. He will look at her kindness as a weakness. He will see her innocence as naiveté and exploit it. He will eventually corrupt the heart of a perfectly good woman.

At the end of the day, it all comes back to pride. Black women must desire a guy who takes pride in being a good man. The type of guy who understands everything he has is a gift from God. Not a self-proclaimed "self-made" man who thinks he made it all happen. Find a man who has a *real* relationship with God, a man who refuses to cheat on you not for fear of losing you, but for fear of losing himself.

Seek a man who knows God's words and lives by His decree, a man who will provide security and protection. Stop searching for security in a label: boyfriend, fiancé, husband and take solace in the content of a man's character. If you had to practically force him to commit to you, your chances of him being faithful are pretty bleak.

162

Labels are a false sense of security, no different than spyware on your computer or a security system in your home. If a professional hacker or thief wants to bypass your firewall or front door he will. But having that protection provides you with a comfort that allows you to sleep at night. If a man is a cheater, no matter the title, he will cheat.

It's a dangerous place to be in a relationship with a man whose monogamy is predicated on his feelings. He is unstable. And so will the relationship be as you go up and down the emotional roller coaster. A man with the right character requires no label. He's not searching for a loophole in the agreement. He's naturally content being with one woman. His loyalty is not established by the relationship. It's deeply-rooted in his principles.

Ultimately, who you decide to allow in your life will impact your personality. Different people bring out a different side of you. You will be influenced by their character to either strive to be greater or be content with life as it is.

Find Your MVP

Growing up in Chicago in the early nineties, I witnessed greatness at its best in the form of "His Airness," otherwise known as Michael Jeffrey Jordan or simply MJ. Watching Jordan play was like a perpetual cliché of poetry in motion. It was like a run-on superlative; he was the bestest. With every move he made you became a prisoner of the moment prone to hyperbole, convinced nothing could ever top what you just witnessed until Jordan palmed the ball again, stuck out his tongue and did something even more ridiculous. We were spoiled by his dominance. We expected to win every game and for every shot he took to go in.

Did Jordan have off nights? Yes. Were there times when he didn't score? Sure. Could we make the argument, on occasion, that Jordan lost us the game? Absolutely! But here is the reality. Every Bulls fan understood that Jordan was the most valuable player, and as he went, so went the team. More often than not he led us to victory. Therefore, in defeat how could we ever blame him for losing? No matter the stakes. If not for his efforts, we wouldn't even be in the position to miss a game-winner. That's the level of excellence you want in a significant other, someone who is a winner even in defeat. <u>Someone you can trust to lead.</u> <u>Someone who makes you better…categorically.</u>

Be Persistently Patient

Finding Mr. Right can be a difficult feat; however, if done right it's done once, and your efforts will last a lifetime. Don't be anxious or allow your aspirations to cloud your better judgement. Instead continue to be persistently patient, working diligently toward your goal of marriage, trusting in God and in your preparation. No matter what, don't rush and don't settle.

 Rushing to the altar only provides temporary happiness. If you think finding a mate is hard now, try marrying the wrong person, having kids, divorcing and starting all over as a thirty-six-year-old divorcee with two kids. <u>Anything worth having requires a</u>

lot of effort and patience. Stay the course.

Settling for less than God's excellence is always a recipe for misfortune. First, it puts you out of alignment with God's will for your life, exposing you to the dangers that go along with walking outside of God's divine path. Second, it opens you up for regrets. I've yet to meet the person who has settled without regrets. Over time regrets manifest into resentment and resentment, once full grown, results in the death of a relationship.

Don't grow impatient and desire *any* kind of love. Patiently wait for the love you deserve. Understand, Rome wasn't built in a day. But also acknowledge the fact that the Romans worked tirelessly all day and night until the job was complete. Patience doesn't mean stand still. It means respect the process.

Be Realistic

Most women want a man who is successful, even if she, herself, brings little to the table. Be realistic with your relationship goals. Your inability to self-assess can be problematic. Too many women have a "what's in it for me?" mentality. Instead ask yourself "What do I have to offer?" If you are a professional underachiever, don't expect to woo a career overachiever. He will notice your flaws from a mile away—no matter how beautiful you are. Your beauty cannot compensate for the flaws in your character. It will simply allow some men to better tolerate you. Remember, being tolerated and being loved are very different things. If you are looking for love avoid dating anyone you believe is out of your league. Inherently, you'll be willing to do anything to please him. The thought is "If I don't do this he's going to move on to the next girl who will." The reality is that he's likely to move on regardless.

If the goal is to capture a rich man, continue spending all your money on clothes, hair and makeup. Frequent the local wine bars where rich men hang out and keep fishing for your shark. But if your goal is to find love, someone who will celebrate you instead of simply tolerate you, understand your market value. Lofty goals limit many women from love.

Some people will take my words out of context, so I want to be sure to make the distinction between self-worth and market value. Self-worth is internal. It's the opinion you have about yourself and the value you place on yourself. It should be completely independent of any outside influences. However, market value is external. It's the opinion others have of you and your value in the marketplace. If we view Black dating as a market, your market value is dictated by the consumer (Black men), no different than any other U.S. consumer market.

Simply stated, your market value is based on supply and demand. How many of you exist in the marketplace? How much demand is there for someone with your qualities? Are you a cookie-cutter commodity? If I lined you up next to a hundred women are you unidentifiable among the masses? Or will you stand out in the crowd? Are you that rare talent like Oprah Winfrey who is a one-woman monopoly? If you're a commodity, you don't dictate your value, the market does. However, if you're a monopoly you have no competition, thus you create your own market value.

Keep It Tight

For those who didn't get the memo, fit is the new sexy. More than ever, Black women are flocking to the gym to preserve, regain or refine their sexy. Gone are the days of the slender stick-figure standard. Black women are in the gym accentuating their natural curves and Black men can't get enough of them. As shallow as it may sound, in this competitive dating marketplace, being severely overweight or out of shape can hinder your chances for love. Men are visual creatures. A woman's appearance is the first thing a man sees. He will quickly size you up and determine whether or not there is interest. If so, what kind? How much? Obviously, the way a woman is dressed or how she carries herself can peak interest, but the initial deciding factor will surely be physical attraction.

Attraction doesn't mean a woman has to be drop-dead gorgeous. It simply means the man has to find her attractive. I concede that some men prefer women with more meat on their bones. Still these women are expected to carry their weight well, with a flattering waist to hip ratio. Thanks to social media sites like Instagram providing the platform to share and pyramid marketing fitness challenges providing cult-like encouragement, it feels as if the whole world is dieting and exercising. Like most, I assumed it was a fad that would fade, but it appears the fitness craze is here to stay for the long haul.

Granted, physical attraction alone will not keep a man. A woman has to have substance. Her conversation has to be deeper than whether or not her shoes match her outfit. However, based on your appearance you may never get to the point of a conversation. I'm madly in love with the internal beauty of my wife, but her athletic build is what first attracted me to her.

Not to be understated is good health, the true blessing of being fit. Obesity in the Black community is a quiet killer. Portion control in soul food cooking is usually dictated by what all can fit on one plate. As a result, type II diabetes and high blood pressure, two diseases linked to obesity, are disproportionately affecting the Black community—especially Black women.

Probably the biggest gain from "keeping it tight" is that you progress through this dating process healthy and feeling good about yourself, which should help give you the confidence to move on if the health of the relationship doesn't match your wellness standards.

Be Uniquely You

In the past I've been asked "What's your type?" by more women than I can count. My answer remains unchanged. "I don't have a type." Truly I do, but relative to the superficial context in which the question was typically being posed, I don't. There is no particular height, weight, skin tone, hair length or body shape that attracts me. I'm attracted to uniqueness. That's my type. Every woman I've dated has been beautiful in her own way. I don't compare and contrast looks. A woman's beauty is just like artwork. Art is not meant to be measured, but rather appreciated. I adored the uniquely beautiful aspects of them all individually.

Don't worry about making yourself available. Make yourself remarkable. Remarkable women are hard to miss. Unremarkable women are easy to forget. You will never be remarkable by tailoring your personality to a man. Don't be a chameleon. Be you, enough with the "me toos."

To borrow a line from Shakespeare "To thine own self be true." Be authentically you whether he finds your quirks and idiosyncrasies appealing or irritating. You can only be on stage for so long. At some point you will get exhausted and start showing kinks in the armor as your true self starts to emerge. Or you will attain your goal of marriage and live unhappily ever after.

Just Say "Hi"

Some years back, Leanne and I went on a cruise to celebrate our anniversary. It was a week-long tour of several of the Caribbean's westernmost islands. About the fifth day, everyone was called down to the auditorium of the ship for a mandatory safety briefing. Our next scheduled stop was Ocho Rios, Jamaica. The crew wanted to make sure everyone who planned to leave the ship understood the rules of engagement when interacting with the locals.

"Don't talk to anyone unless you're interested in buying something," one crew member said emphatically.

169

"If possible, try to avoid eye contact all together." Another crew member added.

Is it really that serious? I thought.

It wasn't until the ship docked and we walked down the ramp into a sea of street merchants that I fully understood the gravity of the situation. I found myself relying on my safety training as we attempted to work our way through the makeshift marketplace at the foot of the dock. It's hard to ignore people when they are coming at you from every direction. But with a stiff neck and eyes fixed on the horizon, I clinched my wife's hand and we made our way to the other side.

This passive-aggressive strategy of eluding people is not limited to the Jamaican marketplace. Here in America, Black women have mastered the art. They use it quite successfully in avoiding potential husbands. If statistics suggest 42 percent of Black women are unwed, why would they deliberately avoid interacting with Black men?

It would require the use of a scientific calculator to count how many times a day I cross paths with a Black woman: work, church, gym, store and she won't even make eye contact, let alone say, "Hi." As a married man, it doesn't bother me because I'm only attempting to be cordial. However, if I were single and looking for a partner, this interaction, or lack thereof, would be very disheartening. If you're single, why ignore men like you're taken?

On the surface, Black women's behavior appears rude and standoffish; but their actions are not without reason. Contrary to popular belief, we don't live in a society full of bitter and angry Black women. This anti-social behavior is simply a defense mechanism. From the point they leave the house until they return home, Black women are bombarded by Black men approaching them from every direction. As a result, Black men's uniqueness has been watered down. We are merely viewed as a bunch of street merchants unidentifiable among the masses? We might have a different pitch, but we're all selling the same thing. Thus, there is no motivation for Black women to want to entertain a conversation.

If I am accurate in capturing Black women's perspective, how do we change the general opinion? More importantly, how do we restore the institution of marriage within the Black community? The lines of communication between Black men and women have to improve. One simple suggestion I have for all the single Black ladies out there is to "Just Say Hi."

Obviously, there is a risk in speaking, it's a delicate waltz Black women dance when choosing to engage with Black men, because there are some egotistical, and self-absorbed Black men out there who will interpret your "Hi" as something greater. Even worse, there are unstable Black men who resort to verbal abuse or violence when women reject their advances. However, we cannot live in fear. If it is something more, continue to explore the possibilities. If not, promptly and sternly end the conversation and wait for the next prospect.

This trial-by-error approach can bring about a lot of headaches, as you will come in contact with all sorts of personalities. But I see no other way to address the issue. While unpleasant at times, it's a necessary sacrifice for the greater good of the Black community. If the trend continues down this path, the number of unwed Black women will grow from 42 percent to 62 percent in the blink of an eye. So if not for you, do it for all your fellow single ladies out there.

Leave Your Bags at the Door

Friction and growing pains are common in new relationships. Much of which is caused by baggage brought in from previous relationships: keeping the line of communication open with an ex, or getting burned and keeping all other men at a distance. You cannot allow your past to negatively impact your future. In relationships you have to enter into every situation with the mindset that you're going to allow yourself to be vulnerable enough to be hurt again. Otherwise, you are carrying reservations and not allowing yourself to be open. Relationships are a risk, sometimes the greater you risk, the greater you are rewarded. You have to be willing to fall in love or fall on your face. And in the words of the great Maya Angelou "Have enough courage to trust love one more time and always one more time."

Relationships are tough. Women are even tougher. In some instances women give their love to a man who only gives his time. When he leaves, she still finds a way to pick up the pieces and move forward—scared but unbroken. Men could never be so resilient. We can be extremely guarded and emotionless. We get burned one time and vow to never trust a woman ever again!

There are good reasons why most relationship experts suggest taking time after a break-up to heal rather than run into the arms of someone else—especially after a long-term relationship. Self-reflection is key in the healing process. But it demands time to analyze what went wrong, but also what was right. Introspection helps prevent you from bringing old baggage into a new relationship. Sometimes the old baggage is you!

Maybe your last boyfriend was verbally abusive, rather than build you up, all he did was tear you down. His constant cheating left you wondering "why am I not good enough?" It wreaked havoc on your self-esteem, causing you to become insecure. Your lack of confidence makes you seek validation from your significant other. When it's not provided, or at least given in a way you think suitable, it feels like rejection, reinforcing your belief that you must not be beautiful enough, good enough, or worthy enough.

Your significant other should absolutely make you feel beautiful, special, and valued. But confidence comes from within. If you often shrink in a room full of beautiful women, it's a reflection of a poor self-image. Putting undue pressure on your man to overcompensate for your inferiority complex is a heavy burden that will wear thin over time.

Sometimes the issue is not a recent ex and requires a much deeper look into your past. Sometimes the problem stems from a childhood of neglect from your father—or maybe even your mother. If no one else on this earth shows love and genuine care for your wellbeing, at least you can rely on your mother and father... right? There is no greater pain than the feeling of being unwanted by a parent. Dealing with the resentment caused by the rejection from a father requires healing. It's easier said than done for sure. Overcoming it is a process. There are necessary steps you must take in order to successfully move forward with your life. Many women attempt to circumvent the process and find themselves years later face-to-face with their daddy issues.

Often we only pay attention to visible injury, but what is sometimes more harmful is the unseen. If you fell and scraped your knee on the concrete and it started to bleed, you would probably clean it and cover it with a bandage. Truthfully, had you done nothing to treat the scrape it would have scabbed up and healed on its own. Now let's say you were in a minor car accident and unknowingly suffered blunt force trauma to the abdomen area, causing severe damage to an internal organ. If you made the mistake of going home rather than to an emergency room, because there was no visible signs of injury, you could potentially die in a matter of hours due to internal bleeding. Some of you are living with emotional internal bleeding and the longer it takes you to receive proper treatment, the more damage it will cause to your health, well-being, and happiness.

If you grew up without a father in the home, you likely grew up being disappointed by your dad, which in turn "taught" you that most men disappoint. Once you started dating, you interacted with most men expecting them to disappoint you as well. This pessimistic view of Black men will literally have you waiting for something bad to happen in your relationship. You will question the motive of a man and create a guilty until proven innocent dating environment.

Maybe addressing these issues is not something you can tackle alone and will require help from a [spiritual] professional. The amount of women turning to alcoholism rather than face the pain of a dysfunctional childhood is troubling. Alcohol only leads to regrets. It often gives women the courage to behave uncharacteristically. You owe it to yourself to invest the time and money needed to become whole. Failure to deal with the problem doesn't make it disappear; it only makes it manifest itself in different, sometimes tragic ways.

Don't Fall for the Banana in the Tailpipe

Many women's biggest problem is that they underestimate the intelligence of men. I hear all the time how women are more clever and how they cheat better, but men can be very calculated—especially when they think they're being underestimated.

I drove a lot of women crazy back in the day, because they couldn't figure out what box to put me in. I wasn't a blatant asshole that signaled "stay away," nor was I the clingy guy who would sniff up behind them and end up in the friend zone. I was career-focused and driven. I was fun, smart and charming. I had a lot of positive characteristics, which led some women to think, "If I could only tweak these couple areas…" What they didn't know was that everything I did had a purpose. I would give a woman just enough to keep her wanting me without obsessing. If I felt more tenderness or toughness was needed to get us back to our off-centered equilibrium, I did what was necessary. Essentially, she was chasing after a carrot she could never catch.

Often women fall into the trap of attempting to mold a man. You see someone with great potential and begin pouring into him. Some men require a little tender loving care to help bring out their absolute best. I'm ten times the man of my youth as a result of my wife's influence. It's natural to desire to be a source of inspiration and encouragement to our mates. But here is where it gets tricky. Change is not a contingency of love. If you cannot accept a man for who he is at present then end the relationship and find a new candidate. Ask yourself "if no aspects about him change can I still embrace him wholeheartedly?" If the answer is "no," you are setting yourself up for failure.

175

Core characteristics of a man will only deviate marginally from its equilibrium. If a man is naturally lacking drive, your shoulder pressed against his back nudging him forward will only carry him so far. As a matter of fact, over time it will have an adverse effect and he will begin to resist and resent you. Your significant other is the person you're supposed to be most comfortable with, not feel like you are constantly proving yourself to. That will grow old and tiresome.

Accept a man for who he is, not for who he could be. Don't attempt to truncate his maturation process. Be patient. Scientific studies suggest that the brain of a female human develops faster than a male from birth through puberty, late adolescence, possibly even until their mid to late twenties. This can cause some men to have lingering immaturity well into their thirties. Never make excuses for him. Always challenge him to be better, but leave room for natural growth. Most importantly, give him unconditional love throughout.

Don't Confuse Routine with Commitment

There are very few memories I have of my brief NFL stint. However, the first day created a lasting memory. I will never forget the first day the shuttle bus dropped the rookies off at Valley Ranch in Irving, TX, for our first day at Cowboy rookie minicamp. I remember walking into the training facility and looking up. There painted on the wall in bold Cowboy blue letters were the words: Don't Confuse Routine with Commitment. Strategically placed at the entrance of the facility by [then] Head Coach, Bill Parcels, it was one of his "isms" to serve as a daily reminder to players that effort is required! You can get into the routine of doing an act over and over until monotony sets in and you start going through the motions. However, if you are committed to being a winner and a champion, every day you work to get better. If you do that you'll maximize the potential of every moment.

The same holds true for relationships. Simply because a man routinely calls and visits doesn't necessarily mean he is committed. What else does he do? Is he consistent with his behavior? Does he follow through on his promises? Does he go out of his way to acknowledge you hold a special place? Effort is not optional. It's a requirement! Effort is the truest reflection of significance. Those who find themselves constantly clamoring for more are overlooking the apparent. If the sum of your relationship isn't greater than your individual effort, you're in a net-loss relationship. Don't let pride cloud your better judgment. Some women will exhaust every excuse before accepting the reality he is just not that interested.

Obey the Law

The law of conservation of energy is a basic law of physics as well as dating. The law states that in an isolated system "energy can neither be created nor destroyed." It is merely transformed from one form to another. When two people enter into a relationship they form a closed system. From the beginning, the energy within that relationship (system) is fixed. One cannot manufacture more energy and force it into the relationship. If energy is lacking at the start, energy will be lacking in the end.

Some people confuse the transformation of energy with the

creation of it; but understand no new energy is being created. Whether it's a new relationship that is starting to blossom or an old one that has rekindled, what you are experiencing is potential energy, or energy at rest, transforming into kinetic energy, or energy in motion. The energy was always there it just needed to be tapped into.

Many new relationships with high energy potential never come to fruition due to one or both parties' inability to make time for dating. They are hard pressed to find time to fit it into their "busy schedules," therefore potential energy remains potential. Energy at rest stays at rest. However, once activated, energy in motion tends to stay in motion. Sometimes your relationship just needs a spark. However, if your relationship is lacking sufficient energy, don't bang your head against a wall trying to defy science. Find a new relationship with greater energy potential.

No Pin the Tail on the Donkey

The intent is not to tell Black women how to approach their sex lives. I share this information with you, in love, for the same reason I shared it with my sister many years ago—to make you aware. Depending on how and where you were raised, you may suffer from a degree of naiveté. Life may have been presented to you sunny side up. The depths of man's deception might be difficult for you to comprehend. Growing up on the south side of Chicago, I was surrounded by vultures who circled the perimeters in search of girls showing any signs of weakness.

I worried about my sister. Even though she was a year older than me, I always viewed her as my little sister. I tried to watch over her, but I knew she had to see the world for herself, so I broke the man code and armed her with information about the game. I even shared stories about my best friend and our wild escapades. I knew she viewed me as one of the good guys. I wanted her to know just how dirty all guys have the potential to be. It was my only way to truly protect her. Unlike women in other cultures, Black women are the least protected, making them the most vulnerable.

I wasn't trying to stop my sister from having fun. My goal was to make her fully aware of her surroundings; that way if she chose to be promiscuous, she would have made a conscious decision. It wouldn't be because some guy tricked her out of her panties.

Asking young Black women today to practice abstinence is like asking today's farmer to use the cotton gin. It sounds awfully old fashion, but if you want a surefire way to be certain a man's intentions are pure and properly aligned, eliminate sex. It will undoubtedly end all the guesswork. The dating mask will peel off quickly. A man cannot sustain a hidden agenda in the face of celibacy. You won't even have to say a word; he will grow impatient and eventually bow out. Many men aren't looking for a relationship; they are searching for the path of least resistance. Their interest in you is not your brilliance. They are entertaining you because you are convenient.

For the more stubborn women, these men will keep the full-court press on until you surrender the cookie, attempting to sleep with you every time they are in your presence. Just keep reminding yourself that the pressure is not real. It's man-ufactured. Some Black men will try to create a pressured envi-ronment, forcing you to turn them down time and time again, hoping your feeling of letting him down will guilt you into bed. You have to become comfortable with an unapologetic "No!"

Given the obvious conflict of interest, most men will not ad-mit to the fact that sex functions as a timestamp in a relationship. The first time you sleep together moves the relationship from the digging stage to the "dig-in" or dinner bell stage—assuming the sex was enjoyable for both parties. Digging to learn more about the woman fades, if not stops all together. It truly depends on a man's intentions for you.

Once you reach the "dig-in" stage everything beyond sex is just foreplay: going to dinner, going to the movies, taking a walk in the park, or something as simple as talking on the phone prior to seeing each other. In a man's mind, he is seasoning you for sex at some point later in the day. Sex dominates his thoughts leaving little room for him to explore deeper levels of you as a person. If you don't believe me, try giving up the cookie on the first date. Then, watch how bent out of shape he becomes if he can't get more on dates two and three. On second thought... don't! Once sex is introduced, men understand that many wom-en would prefer not to have a slew of sex partners, so the odds are in his favor that you will continue to come to him for your sexual needs.

Even men hoping to settle down will use sex to test and see if you are, in fact, wifey material. Men understand that a woman's relationship with sex is a direct reflection of her self-respect. Many men fear marrying a woman who may be monogamously

180

challenged. The #1 rule in the man code book is "never turn a hoe into a housewife." When men get married, it's usually because they're ready to settle down and have kids. The last concern a man wants when his wife gets pregnant is if the child is his. Casual sex is a definite red flag that will likely demote you to the homie-lover-friend zone. Putting you through a test is a win-win proposition. If he tests you and you pass, the relationship can continue down the serious path. If he tests you and you fail...well at least he separated the real from the fake and got some booty as consolation.

Many people view sex as this overpowering act of spontaneous passion that randomly occurs between a man and woman without regards for relationship or comfort level. The problem with that animalistic outlook on sex is that we are not dogs. We are human beings with far more sophisticated brains, and complex thoughts and feelings. Sex creates a spiritual and emotional attachment—especially for women. We take a little bit of each sex partner with us as we journey through life. The effects of mounting sex partners add to the burden of baggage we carry into new relationships. Beyond the emotional toll there are obvious risk factors involved with casual sex which should further discourage anyone from treating it as a random act.

Even within the confines of a new relationship sex can muddy the waters. Having sex too soon often creates a dynamic whereby the relationship gets measured by how much sex you're having and how good it is. Lack of sex implies the demise of the relationship. But the reality is that responsibilities will sometimes interfere and over time passion in the bedroom will wane.

Hold off on sex for as long as possible (and trust me, you can go longer than you think). Spend quality time learning about each other. Become friends first. Over the course of a relationship and definitely a marriage, sex will be such a small portion of how you spend your time together. If you don't enjoy the individual, no matter how much you enjoy the sex it will not sustain the relationship.

Put sex in its proper place. Don't give it power over you or your relationship. Contrary to popular belief, sex is a want not a need. Unlike water, you won't die if you ain't gettin' none. It truly boils down to a philosophical question of whether you would rather never have sex or never find love.

Remember, the sex drive is in the brain not the groin. Though some physical attributes can increase sexual arousal, actual pleasure comes from the significance of the person—especially for women. If there is no emotional connection, the likelihood of being pleasured is slim. The key to great sex is finding love.

Find Your Love Language (and His)

The 5 Love Languages: The Secret to Love that Lasts is a phenomenal relationship book written by Christian author and marriage counselor Dr. Gary Chapman. The premise is that we love in different languages. Chapman suggests there are five types of love languages: Words of Affirmation, Quality Time, Receiving Gifts, Acts of Service and Physical Touch. Chapman also notes we tend to love others in our own love language, causing affection to sometimes get lost in translation. Learning to be multilingual can be the difference between a relationship surviving or dying.

I was first introduced to this book during premarital counseling. Leanne and I were given a blank sheet of paper and asked to rank each other's love languages in descending order. Leanne took several minutes. However, I was done in an instant convinced that I knew my soon-to-be spouse inside and out. As you can imagine, like most people who are overconfident, I failed miserably. I possibly had one right out of five. It was an eye-opening and somewhat alarming exercise. Here we were months away from tying the knot and I had no fundamental understanding of how my fiancé wanted to be loved. I started taking pre-marital counseling far more seriously. I discovered that she loves Words of Affirmation most of all and that receiving gifts paled in comparison to the rest of her languages.

But even that was fluid, not at all engraved in stone. Over time, her primary language has changed. With the birth of children and all the subsequent work they demand, Acts of Service supplanted Words of Affirmation as her number one love language. In other words, she doesn't need any more rah-rah speeches. She needs me to roll up my sleeves and get to work on the pile of dirty dishes.

Pick and Choose Your Battles

Unless you're one of those women who loves to break up for the make up, arguing and fighting isn't fun. You would much rather be cuddling and watching a movie with your man rather than playing a game of silent treatment. If there are issues in your relationship that need to be addressed, by all means make him aware. But don't add fuel to the fire. If the subject is trivial don't give it energy. Dispose of it quickly and preserve your happiness. By "trivial" I'm referring to arguments over issues that are insignificant to the relationship.

For instance, the notorious "Who had the remote last?" argument. You would be surprised at the inordinate amount of energy expended over something so frivolous. Don't waste your time. Focus on habitual problems or issues with far reaching implications. Those are the ones worth digging in your heels over—no matter how major or minor. If your significant other periodically gets upset during arguments and balls up his fist as if he's going to strike you then walks away, that is absolutely not a sign you want to ignore.

Address the problem head-on. However, don't be so concerned with winning the argument that you lose sight of your purpose. Men have a tendency to jump on the defense and the whole exercise will become unproductive. The goal is to help him understand the error of his ways without personal attacks or rendering him voiceless. There may be some underlying problems in the relationship that are triggering his unbecoming behavior. Whether perception or reality, but never an excuse for violence, often times a man becomes angry with his partner because he feels somehow disrespected. Learn how to finesse your approach to help get to the heart of the problem. A passive-aggressive approach can be just as effective—if not more. Rather than attempt to match his intensity, tug at his heartstrings. Think of examples and analogies that he can relate to. If he's a sports fan, use a sports analogy. If he's a business man, use a business analogy. Help him understand the problem from your point of view. Don't force feed him thoughts then wonder why he hasn't corrected his actions. It's because you haven't convinced him that his actions are the problem.

Prepare to Submit

By far, one of the most difficult concepts for today's Independent Black Woman to grasp, is submission and accepting her role as Black man's helpmate. On paper, many Black women are willing to follow their man until it's time for execution. Following a man's lead goes against all the current rhetoric of the New-Age Black Feminist Movement. The single greatest opposition is the negative connotation surrounding the word "submit", which creates a misconception that submission is synonymous with weakness. If you equate submission to weakness and you view yourself as a strong Black woman, then being submissive to a man will surely infringe upon your strength as a woman and you will reject it. However, the act of spiritual submission doesn't require women to surrender any power.

Contrary to popular belief, helpmate doesn't mean subordinate or "property of." Some wives have internalized this belief causing them to resist taking their husband's last name. They are fighting to preserve a false sense of independence; but this resistance has long-term consequences.

Woman was created with power equal to, but also opposite of man's. She was designed to be man's complement, perfectly possessing all the qualities he lacks. Her intrinsic power comes from her natural ability to fill a void in man. A woman's love can heal any man's heart and nurture him back from the depths of despair. That's the true essence of a woman.

The belief that gender roles are obsolete is a lie; no matter how often society attempts to force feed it to us. God created man and woman for a specific purpose. This purpose stretches far beyond learned domestic roles of human beings. Yes, men and women alike can cook and clean, as well as take out the trash, or fix leaky faucets. However, man and woman's innate roles are spiritually (Biblically) and physically (scientifically) assigned.

By innate biological makeup, women have ovaries that produce eggs, making them the designated child-bearers. Thus, women inherently are more nurturing (and catering) than men. On the other hand, men have higher levels of testosterone, making them stronger and more aggressive than women. Therefore, men are instinctively more protective than women. As a result, men need to be nurtured and women need to feel protected. These are not learned behaviors. They are the fabric of what makes us male and female. However, we live in a liberal society today that will argue, "It's due time that men carry babies!" all in the name of gender equality.

If the goal is to truly eliminate gender roles, why aren't more Black women dropping to one knee proposing to their boyfriends? Surely this would help reduce the amount of single-parent homes. Women shouldn't advocate to remove gender roles only when it is convenient. If you're uncomfortable with the idea of proposing to your man, it's because part of you fundamentally believes men were designed to lead the relationship.

I concede that some Black men have adopted a "worldly" view of submission that is distorted and oppressive. You would be hard pressed to find a Black man who doesn't feel his woman should allow him to "wear the pants." Often, unqualified men make this appeal, despite having failed to display the capacity to lead—spiritually, financially or physically. He seeks control for all the wrong reasons. He wants the most excellent love even though he's giving the bare minimum. It's akin to "Do as I say and not as I do." This man is not worthy of your submission, as he has not yet submitted himself to God. When a man lacks the ability to lead, the question is not should you follow him. The question is why are you with him?

PARTING
THOUGHTS...

By now you've realized that categorizing *His Dough, Her Cookie* as a relationship book was truly just a guise. Instead of simply providing you with relationship advice, I took you on a historical journey through Black men and women's relationship dynamics from slavery to present day hoping to help us realize that much of our dissension was by design. The better we embrace this fact; the tighter we embrace each other, and refuse to perpetuate the manufactured conflict. This book was written to adults, but it's without question for our children. This message is bigger than one person or one relationship. It's bigger than one neighborhood or one city. It's about the collective consciousness of all Black America. We have to channel our intellectual gifts and help turn this wayward ship back on course. The future of our children depends on it. We cannot *collectively* shout "Black Lives Matter!" in the wake of police brutality against our youth and ignore how our *division* has left our communities vulnerable to predatory policing.

With Black America already generations behind in wealth accumulation compared to our White counterparts, choosing to remain single instead of joining forces in marriage is further widening the wealth gap and hindering economic growth within the Black community. As a result, many Black children are being subjected to a similar ascribed status that our generation was born into. Just as our ancestors paved the way for us, we must press forward with great deliberateness striving to leave the Black community better than we inherited it. We progress the Black community by restoring the Black family...one healthy marriage at a time.

Beyond more strong Black marriages and more Black fathers' presence at home, it absolutely takes a village to raise a child. Unfortunately, within the Black community that village has become non-existent. Back in the day, if someone in the community witnessed a child doing something inappropriate, the child was immediately reprimanded and a smoke signal was sent out to the parents to inform them before they even arrived home from work. The community doesn't operate the same way today—partly because the younger generations interact more in cyberspace than face-to-face. When I was growing up the whole neighborhood considered everything happening in the community as their business. In turn, this "village" helped to raise the children in the community.

Now, more than ever, we've become a "picket-fence" society choosing to focus our attention on our own backyards and turn a blind eye to the problems that exist on the other side of the fence. However, often in community living, we live communally as a neighborhood. What separates us also connects us to the rest of the community. If my neighbor decides to turn his backyard into a pistol range, for obvious reasons my focus could not remain isolated. Having a pistol range next door, with three small children, would make playing in the backyard extremely dangerous. Issues on the outside seem to always find a way of seeping into our coveted private spaces. If we better understand that problems affecting the whole impacts the individual, the concern becomes more heightened—if for no other reason than self-preservation. A wise man once said, "We are caught in an inescapable network of mutuality, tied in a single garment of destiny. Whatever affects one directly, affects all indirectly." Those are the profound words of Dr. Martin Luther King Jr.

People don't exist in a vacuum—especially Black people. In fact, more often than not, Black people are clustered together in pockets of poverty throughout urban America. The rest are scattered throughout White suburbia strengthening its economy. We hear much about "White flight," but it's Black flight, the move of Black city-dwellers to the suburbs to escape dangerous Black neighborhoods, that has decimated the Black community. White suburbs are as much of a status symbol as they are a safe haven. Like most of my friends, I was reared to believe that success meant making it out of the projects—out of my neighborhood. Just about everyone's goal is to get out. By virtue, those who are left behind are viewed as underachievers. Those who are successful in their quest often never look back. What is left is a Black community devoid of people with the education and capital to uplift it.

In the few major cities with affluent Black communities: D.C., Atlanta, Raleigh, and Charlotte, there are barriers within the broader Black community separating the haves from the have-nots. Though, the reality for Black people is that we are all the have-nots. We are all lacking. Regardless of class, there are certain freedoms that no amount of money can grant—privileges reserved only for Whites. We must stop living in fear of each other, retreating to predominately White suburbs for safety. We all say we want "better" for our kids, but subjecting them to an environment where no one looks like them hardly constitutes better. I want the most enriching experience for my children as possible. This goes far beyond school

193

ratings and median incomes. There is a sociocultural component that is equally as important, one that no leafy gated community in White suburbia can cultivate.

I understand that fear is not always the motive. Black folks choose to live in predominately White suburbs for the same reason Black students flock to Private White Institutions, (PWIs) in lieu of Historically Black Colleges and Universities (HBCUs), it's where all the resources are kept. I have children; I understand. However, I also realize that this Black flight model will never fix the fiscal problem in Black America. It only depletes a community of its natural resources.

What if successful Black folks decided to stay put and build up their own communities? Where would the resources be? What if the thousands of exploited collegiate football and basketball players, who are predominately Black, decided to take their talents to HBCUs instead of PWIs? Where would the lucrative network contracts reside? We have more power than we think, if we can only unify.

In the early 1900s, a small neighborhood in Tulsa, Oklahoma named Greenwood became famous for its thriving Black-owned businesses. Greenwood built a financial blueprint that would later earn it the nickname "Black Wall Street." Due to segregation laws, Blacks were not permitted to patronize any White establishments. This forced Blacks to create their own clothing stores, restaurants, schools, newspapers and hotels. Greenwood enjoyed unprecedented success until the Tulsa Race Riot of 1921. Hundreds were massacred and much of the Greenwood neighborhood was destroyed by fires. However, contrary to popular belief, fire didn't ruin Black Wall Street, desegregation did. Despite the deliberate acts of hate

194

committed against them, Greenwood citizens rebuilt the community, but when Blacks were allowed to take their money and spend it elsewhere, they did. Black dollars have been cycling outside of the Black community ever since. That money must find its way back home.

I'm not bashful about my declaration. Why should I be when a city like Chicago, with a high-gliding murder rate, can justify spending over fifty million dollars to build an outdoor concert hall downtown to give tourists the impression of a majestic oasis, when a few miles southwest of the city is dark and desolate, devoid of most city resources and investments? If not us, then who? If not now, then when?

Ironically, the indicators of growth and mobility (e.g., percent below the poverty line, percent who own homes, real median household income) suggest that the ills of Black America have worsened instead of improved under the administration of our first Black president. Obviously, inheriting a nation in a recession combined with deliberate obstruction from Republicans limited his ability to improve the financial position of Black America—with the exception of unemployment. While the Black unemployment rate dropped precipitously, food stamp participation exploded. The correlation suggests that while more Black Americans are back to work, the wages earned leaves many families living below the poverty line. Employment rates alone cannot be the measurement of success. The type of employment and rate of pay matters.

As a race deeply plagued by social injustice and discriminatory hiring practices, we often find ourselves sifting through the numbers to determine if the whole story is being told. We've never measured our success by the standards set forth by White America. Blacks' success, in its purest form, used to be measured by our accomplishments relative to its impact on Black culture. Today, the focus appears to be primarily on individual monetary success. Somewhere along the way the individual success of some Blacks has caused us to lose sight of the disproportionate number of Black Americans still living in abject poverty.

I take no exception to young Black men and women pursuing personal wealth; but there has to be a greater purpose for the wealth other than to flaunt it. That greater purpose should be building wealth for future generations and contributing to the growth and success of the Black community.

As encouraging as it is to watch young Blacks thrive, it's mutually as discouraging to observe how some embrace their success. When did being successful morph into exclusivity—velvet ropes, unlimited bottles of top-shelf liquor, A-list crowds? Blacks' success has never been about exclusivity. It's been about cultural progress and solidarity. If you read about the successful African Americans in our history—W.E.B. Du Bois, Wilma Rudolph, Langston Hughes, George Washington Carver, Fannie Lou Hamer, Mary McLeod Bethune, Muhammad Ali—they all have one thing in common. Their contributions helped advance the African American race. You would struggle to convince me how young Blacks' self-indulgence is helping do the same.

To quote Dr. Cornel West, "Too many young folk have addiction to superficial things and not enough conviction for substantial things like justice, truth and love." We need a deeper awareness of the events happening around us that are impacting the Black community and less focus on celebrity gossip and material gains, which have no bearing on the overall direction and well-being of

196

our community.

We have to get back properly aligned as a culture and a people. We have to return to our spiritual roots and reclaim our identity as children of the Most-High God. We have to reinvest in the black community, and in each other, and take our rightful place in American society as first-class citizens—second to none. We can argue about how we get there, but let's at least have the conversation. As we adjust our lens and change our focus, the outlook for Black America will radically and undoubtedly be changed forever.

IN LOVING MEMORY OF SHERMAN WILLIAM HARRISON

ACKNOWLEDGMENTS

First and foremost, I want to thank God. Each night before I entered my office, before I sat down at my desk, before I powered on my computer, I prayed. I asked God to use me and my words to help reestablish marriage in the Black community. If this book has even the slightest influence on its restoration, all glory and honor is due to my Heavenly Father.

I want to thank my editor, Carol Taylor. You saw the value in my work from day one. Your enthusiasm was evident in all our interactions. You were every bit of what I expected and more. Most of all, you weren't afraid to speak your mind and challenge me when necessary. Your rare blend - of passion and professionalism made you the perfect editor for this project.

I want to thank my designer Denise Billups, who has designed every book I've written thus far. You are an amazing talent. I also want to thank Corey Hanks, Matt Duckett, Georgia Scott and Laura Shelley for their assistance.

Last but not least, I want to thank my wife, business partner and best friend, Leanne, for all she's done to help make this book possible. Your feedback and early reading of the manuscript was invaluable. Your attention to detail in creating the concept for the cover was simply masterful. It's not easy being married to me. Thank you for continuing to lift me up and hold down the fort.

I want to thank my children, Zoe, Caleb and Tori, your mere existence has motivated me to be more and do more. Forgive me for the times when you wanted to play, but Daddy was locked away in the office writing. You don't understand now, but I pray my efforts become evident when you're old enough to read this book. Let my desire to use my voice for good encourage you to do the same in your own special way.

About the Author

TORRI STUCKEY is a native of Chicago (Robbins), IL. A former standout football talent, Torri remains one of Eisenhower High School's (Blue Island, IL) most decorated athletes. Torri continued his football career at the prestigious Northwestern University where he was a four-year letterman, team co-captain and member of the Wildcats' 2000 Big Ten Championship team. After college, he had a brief stint in the NFL with the Dallas Cowboys. In addition to writing books, Torri is a blogger and speaker. When he's not spending time with his wife and three children, he uses his platform to merge his love for writing with his passion for activism. His previous book, *Impoverished State of Mind: Thinking Outside da Block*, has been well received by schools and youth organizations throughout the country. The wide success of *Impoverished State of Mind* has fully cemented Torri's transition from professional athlete to professional author.

How to connect with the author:
>Facebook.com/torristuckey
>Twitter.com/torristuckey
>Instagram: tstuck29

REFERENCES

Abma, J., Chandra, A., Mosher, W., Peterson, L., & Piccinino, L. (1997). *Fertility, family planning, and women's health: New data from the 1995 National Survey of Family Growth*. National Center for Health Statistics. Vital Health Stat, 23(19).

Alexander, M. (2012). *The new Jim Crow: Mass incarceration in the age of colorblindness*. New York: New Press.

Angelou, M. (2009). *Letter to my daughter*. New York: Random House.

Barker, K. L., & Burdick, D. W. (2002). *Zondervan KJV study Bible: Large print King James Version*. Grand Rapids: Zondervan.

Biko, S., & Stubbs, A. (2002). *I write what I like: Selected writings*. Chicago: University of Chicago Press.

Eisenstein, Z. R. (1978). *Capitalist patriarchy and the case for socialist feminism*. New York: Monthly Review Press.

Carson, E.A. (2014). *Prisoners in 2013*. U.S. Department of Justice, Bureau of Justice Statistics, NCJ 247282.

Center for Disease Control (CDC). (2012). *Estimated HIV incidence among adults and adolescents in the United States, 2007–2010*. HIV Surveillance Supplemental Report, 17(4).

Chapman, G. (2004). *The five love languages: How to express heartfelt commitment to your mate*. Chicago: Northfield Publishing.

Cleaver, E. (1991). *Soul on ice*. New York: Random House.

Cruz-Janzen, M. (2007). "Madre Patria (Mother Country): Latino identity and rejections of blackness". Trotter Review: Vol. 17: Iss. 1, Article 6.

Ehrlich, R. (2014). "A permanent family crisis". *National Review*.

Fears, D. (2004). "Black baby boomers' income gap cited". *Washington Post*, A02.

Federal Writers' Project. (1976). *Slave narratives: A folk history of slavery in the United States, from interviews with former slaves*. St. Clair Shores, Mich: Scholarly Press.

Foster, F. S. (2010). *'Til death or distance do us part: Love and marriage in African America*. Oxford: Oxford University Press.

Grandberry, O., Brown, C., & Chilombo, J. (2014). Post to be. *Sex Playlist* [MP3 file]. United States: MMG/Atlantic.

Hamilton BE, Martin JA, Osterman MJK, et al. (2015). *Births: Final data for 2014.* National vital statistics reports; vol 64 no 12. Hyattsville, MD: National Center for Health Statistics.

Haskin, A ., & Aguh, C. "All hairstyles are not created equal: What the dermatologist needs to know about black hairstyling practices and the risk of traction alopecia (TA)". *JAAD.* Vol. 75, Iss. 3.

Houghton, I. (2009). Name of love. *The power of one* [MP3 file]. Mobile, Ala.: Integrity Music.

Hunter, T. (2010). *Slave marriages, Families were often shattered by auction block* (M. Martin, Interviewer) [Audio File]. Retreived from http://www.npr.org/templates/story/story.php? storyId=123608207

Johnson, L.B. (1964). "A battle to build the Great Society". *The Michigan Alumnus.* Bentley Historical Library, University of Michigan.

Joiner, M., & Welner, C. (1942). *Employment of Women in War Production.* Bureau of Employment Security, Reports and Analysis Division.

Knowles, B. (2016). Formation. *Lemonade* [MP3]. New York, NY: Parkwood Entertainment/Columbia

Lyons, C. J., & Pettit, B. (2008). *Compounded disadvantage: Race, incarceration, and wage growth.* Ann Arbor, Mich: National Poverty Center.

Mauer, M., King, R. S., & Sentencing Project (U.S.). (2007). *A 25-year quagmire: The war on drugs and its impact on American society.* Washington, D.C.: Sentencing Project.

Mauer, M., & Sentencing Project (U.S.). (2009). *The changing racial dynamics of the war on drugs.* Washington, DC: Sentencing Project.

McDaniel, A., DiPrete, T. A., Buchmann, C., & Shwed, U. (2011). "The black gender gap in educational attainment: Historical trends and racial comparisons". *Demography, 48*(3), 889-914.

Miller, C. (2014). "The divorce surge is over, but the myth lives on". *NY Times.*

Miller, T. (2011). *Partnering for education reform.* U.S. Department of Education.

Moynihan, D. (1965). *The negro family: The case for national action.* U.S. Department of Labor, Office of Policy Planning And Research.

Nitsche, N.S., & Bruecker, H. (2009). *Opting out of the family? Racial inequality in family formation patterns among highly educated women*. Yale University, Department of Sociology.

Obama, B. (2006). *The audacity of hope: Thoughts on reclaiming the American dream*. New York: Crown Publishers.

Sentencing Project. (2013). *Report of The Sentencing Project to the United Nations Human Rights committee*.

Smith, B., Hull, G. T., & Bell-Scott, P. (1982). *All the women are white, all the blacks are men, But some of us are brave: Black women's studies*. New York: Feminist press.

Social Security Administration. (2001). *Childhood disability: Supplemental security income program*. Publication No. 64-049.

Stuckey, T. (2012). *Impoverished state of mind: Thinking outside da block*. Oak Forest: Cover Three Publishing.

Toldson, I. (2011). "New research shatters myths and provides new hope for black love and marriage". *Empower* Magazine.

Tyler, J., & Lofstrom, M. (2009). "Finishing high school: Alternative pathways and dropout recovery". *The Future of Children* Vol. 19 No. 1.

U.S. Census Bureau (2000). *General Demographic Characteristics:2000*. Washington, DC: U.S. Government Printing Office.

U.S. Census Bureau. (2002). *The big payoff: Educational attainment and synthetic*. Washington, DC: U.S. Government Printing Office.

U.S. Census Bureau. (2012). *The two or more races population: 2010*. Washington, DC: U.S. Government Printing Office.

U.S. Congress, Office of Technology Assessment. (1988). *Infertility: Medical and social choices*. Washington, DC: U.S. Government Printing Office.

Valentine, H. (1838). *A letter from Hannah Valentine to Michael Valentine*, Campbell Family Papers. David M. Rubenstein Rare Book & Manuscript Library, Duke University.

Washington, J. (2010). "Blacks struggle with 72 percent unwed mothers rate". *Associated Press*.

Wilcox, W.B. (2015). "Don't be a bachelor: Why married men work harder, smarter and make more money". *Washington Post*.

Zondervan Publishing House. (2011). *Holy Bible: New International Version*. Grand Rapids: Zondervan.

INDEX

209

CPSIA information can be obtained
at www.ICGtesting.com
Printed in the USA
BVOW09*1243140517
484041BV00002B/15/P